NEWFOUNDLAND & LABRADOR

MICHAEL JOHANSEN

Newmarket Public Library

D1516925

6·32

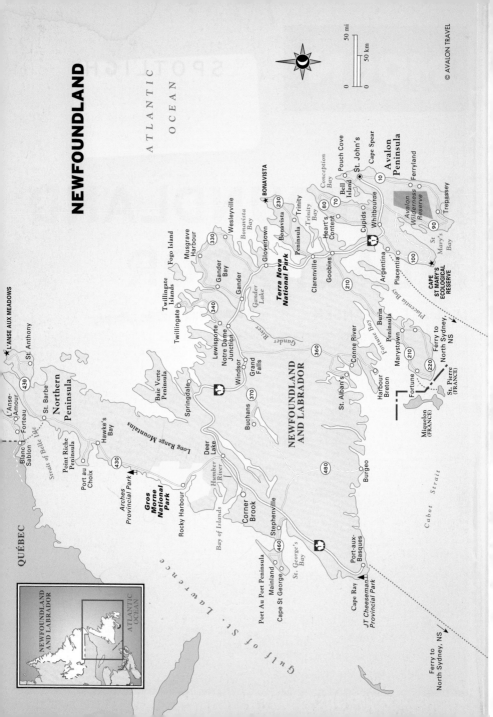

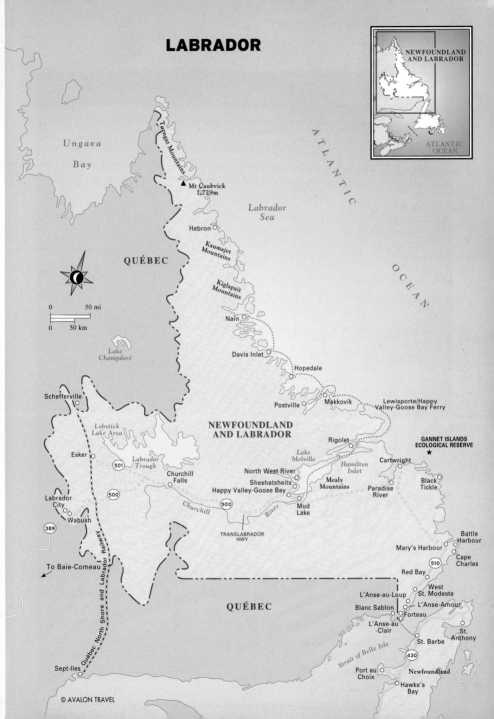

Contents

▶ **Discover Newfoundland & Labrador** **6**

▶ **St. John's and the Avalon Peninsula** **9**
  Sights 13
  Sports and Recreation 18
  Entertainment and Events 19
  Shopping 22
  Accommodations 22
  Food 23
  Information and Services 24
  Getting There and Around 25
  Avalon Peninsula 25

▶ **Central and Western Newfoundland** **31**
  Bonavista and Burin Peninsulas 34
  Terra Nova National Park 37

Gander and Grand Falls-Windsor 39
Iceberg Alley and the
  Great Whale Coast 42
Coast of Bays 46
Deer Lake to Port au
  Port Peninsula 47
Gros Morne National Park 51
Northern Peninsula 57
Port aux Basques and
  the South Coast 61

▶ **Labrador** **63**
  The Straits 66
  Southern Labrador 71
  Happy Valley-Goose Bay
    and Vicinity 77
  Western Labrador 84
  Northern Labrador 88

▶ **Index** **92**

Discover Newfoundland & Labrador

The rugged, rocky island of Newfoundland and the remote but alluring territory of Labrador have long been crossroads for the world, yet they remain largely unknown. Aboriginal peoples lived and thrived on the Rock and across the Big Land thousands of years ago. Norse Vikings explored the treacherous coastlines and tried to settle here over one millenia ago. Basques crossed a wild ocean in tiny wooden boats to hunt great whales in the Strait of Belle Isle. French, Spanish, Portuguese, Irish, and English fisherfolk came to harvest the plentiful cod off the Grand Banks and stayed to raise families in the isolated outports. Today thousands come by boat, plane, and wilderness highway from all over the world to discover the spirit and mystery of Newfoundland and Labrador.

Together Newfoundland and Labrador make up Canada's youngest province, only having joined the country in 1949. Before that it was essentially a semi-independent member of the British Empire. There was a time when its citizens had the choice to become part of the United States, but they opted for Confederation instead. The province is divided geographically, but not politically, into two areas. The island of Newfoundland is about one-quarter the size of Labrador, but it has ten times the population of the mainland territory. Traditionally, both Newfoundlanders and

Labradorians have depended on fishing and forestry for their livelihoods, but today (partially due to the steadily depleting fish stocks and timber stands), the economy is more diversified. Considerable investments are being made to develop oil, mineral, and hydroelectric resources, and to build adequate infrastructure for traveling in and around the province.

No matter how many times you visit or how long you stay, these lands and the people who live here will welcome you and continue to enrich your senses, excite your imagination, and test your taste for adventure. New-foundland and Labrador, carved from the wilderness and battered by the North Atlantic Ocean, are quickly revealed as places of remarkable, enticing, and even dangerous beauty. They are home to a modern and vibrant mix of cultures that has grown out of a long and rich history, but to the wide world Newfoundland and Labrador are mostly known only by name. Because of that — and because of their thousands of kilometers of near-pristine wilder-ness — they remain some of the last frontiers of travel in North America.

ST. JOHN'S AND THE AVALON PENINSULA

The capital city of Newfoundland and Labrador is St. John's, which is built around one of best natural harbours in the world and is counted as one of the oldest surviving European settlements in the Americas. St. John's is the largest city in the province, and as one of the most distinctive in North America, it's certain to be the one place visitors won't miss.

A trip to St. John's will give visitors a sense of history. It is called the City of Legends, after all. The past continues to have a hold on the city of today, from Signal Hill and its place in transatlantic communications to Quidi Vidi Village's rustic buildings, and even the modern Rooms, whose structure is meant to recall traditional fishing buildings of old. That's not to say the city doesn't have a good time—George Street in downtown St. John's is said to have the highest concentration of bars and other nightlife venues of any street on the continent. And come summer, a wide array of festivals celebrate everything from theatre to live music, to folk arts and street performing.

Beyond St. John's, the rest of the Avalon Peninsula is less urban. Provincial parks dot and protect the landscape, small communities preserve traditions—with some even digging up parts of the past—and whales, puffins, and icebergs are coveted views off the coast.

PLANNING YOUR TIME

St. John's has the major airport serving the province, so many visitors headed to Newfoundland and Labrador stop in the city. Whether St. John's is your only destination or one stop of many, there is plenty to keep you busy. During

© PAUL PIGOTT

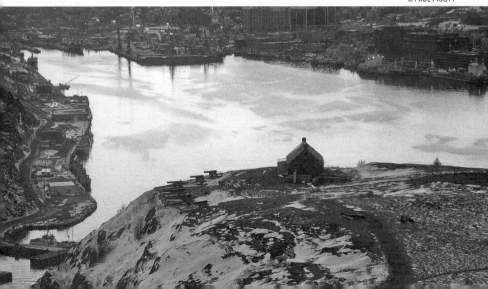

HIGHLIGHTS

◖ Signal Hill: This park perches high above the Narrows and offers amazing views both out to sea and over St. John's Harbour and much of the city (page 13).

◖ Johnson Geo Centre and Geo Park: The centre is a museum of living rock built on Signal Hill to display the geological history of Newfoundland and to show both the past and future of our solar system (page 14).

◖ Quidi Vidi Village: Found on Quidi Vidi Gut below Quidi Vidi Lake a few minutes north of downtown, this St. John's neighborhood retains the look of the fishing outport it was founded as more than 300 years ago (page 14).

◖ The Rooms: Named for Newfoundland and Labrador's traditional style of fishing sheds (which they are built to resemble), this state-of-the-art facility houses the province's archives, art gallery, and museum (page 15).

◖ Cape Spear National Historic Site: The most easterly point on the North American continent is the site of the city's most important lighthouse for more than 175 years (page 17).

◖ George Street: The destination of choice for serious lovers of nightlife, this short pedestrian lane is known for having more bars and nightclubs per square foot than any other street in North America (page 19).

◖ Colony of Avalon: Founded in 1621 at what later became Ferryland, this early English colony was soon destroyed by French raiders and then forgotten. Today the ruins have been uncovered and can be seen by all (page 27).

◖ Cape St. Mary's Ecological Reserve: Made famous in song, this historic point off the southwest Avalon is the protected seasonal home and breeding ground of tens of thousands of migrating seabirds (page 28).

◖ Bell Island: Reached by a frequent ferry not far from St. John's, on this large island in Conception Bay you can explore woods, beaches, and the deep shafts of an abandoned iron ore mine (page 29).

◖ Cupids: This pretty village on Conception Bay has just celebrated its 400th birthday, and visitors can see the archeological site of Canada's first British colony (page 29).

LOOK FOR ◖ TO FIND RECOMMENDED SIGHTS AND ACTIVITIES.

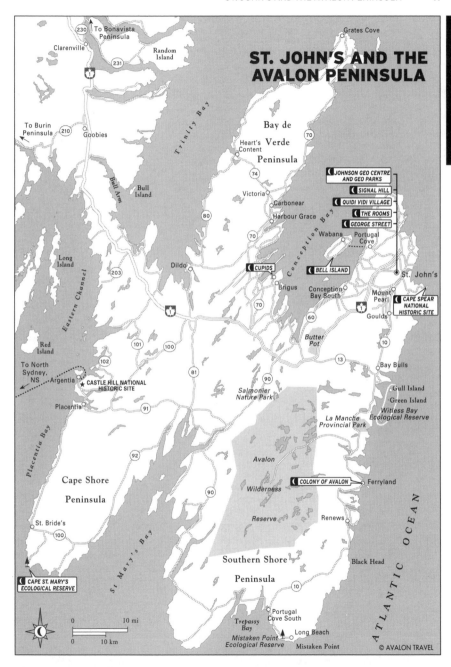

ST. JOHN'S AND THE AVALON PENINSULA

To Bonavista Peninsula
Clarenville
Random Island
Grates Cove

To Burin Peninsula
Goobies

Trinity Bay

Bay de Verde Peninsula

Heart's Content

Victoria

Carbonear
Harbour Grace

Bull Island

Long Island

Dildo

Brigus

Conception Bay

Wabana
Portugal Cove

JOHNSON GEO CENTRE AND GEO PARKS
SIGNAL HILL
QUIDI VIDI VILLAGE
THE ROOMS
GEORGE STREET

CUPIDS

BELL ISLAND

St. John's

Eastern Channel

Red Island

To North Sydney, NS
Argentia

CASTLE HILL NATIONAL HISTORIC SITE

Placentia

Placentia Bay

Conception Bay South

Mount Pearl

Goulds

CAPE SPEAR NATIONAL HISTORIC SITE

Butter Pot

Bay Bulls

Gull Island
Green Island
Witless Bay Ecological Reserve

Salmonier Nature Park

La Manche Provincial Park

Cape Shore Peninsula

Avalon

Wilderness

Reserve

COLONY OF AVALON   Ferryland

Renews

St. Bride's

CAPE ST. MARY'S ECOLOGICAL RESERVE

St Mary's Bay

Southern Shore Peninsula

Black Head

Trepassy Bay
Portugal Cove South
Long Beach

Mistaken Point Ecological Reserve
Mistaken Point

ATLANTIC OCEAN

0   10 mi
0   10 km

© AVALON TRAVEL

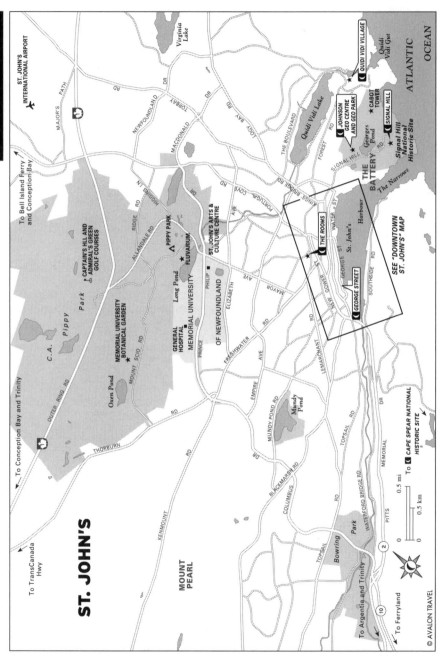

© AVALON TRAVEL

the day, there's Signal Hill, the various historic neighborhoods, city parks, and museums, and at night George Street is the main destination. Even if it's not to your taste, it's worth a stop to get a feel for the experience.

Anyone staying at any of the central hotels or inns can reach most of the city's attractions, shops, restaurants, and nightlife on foot, or by short cab ride. Do keep in mind that the distances may be short around downtown, but the hills can be terribly steep.

Those staying outside the downtown area will have a longer time reaching the city's main attractions and sights, but they have the option of hiring a cab or taking public transit. However, the city's bus system doesn't extend everywhere—in particular it doesn't come close enough to the St. John's airport to do luggage-laden tourists any good.

St. John's can also serve as a base for exploring the rest of the Avalon Peninsula, since all but the farthest ends of the peninsula are within a two-hour drive from the city. You will need a car, though, since the only major bus service doesn't stray from the TransCanada Highway and the most interesting spots are along the loops coming off the TCH. Easy day trips from the city include Bell Island, where you can go to the beach, Witless Bay Ecological Reserve for bird- and whale-watching by boat (some companies can arrange pickups in St. John's), and Ferryland for a glimpse into an early English colony.

Many places in this region, and throughout the province, are only open seasonally. Expect many places to start limiting hours after Labour Day and shutting down completely by early October. Things start to open up again in late April, with the region in full swing by the end of June.

Sights

Orientation

St. John's grew up around its harbour, which slants in a northeast to southwest direction from the Atlantic Ocean. The Narrows is the channel of water that connects the harbour to the ocean. The downtown area hugs the north/west side of the harbour, while Signal Hill rises up above the Narrows. Quidi Vidi Gut is another inlet to the north of the Narrows.

◖ SIGNAL HILL

The best place to start a first (or any) visit to St. John's is on the top of Signal Hill (Signal Hill Road, 709/772-5367, www.pc.gc.ca, visitors centre 10 A.M.–6 P.M. daily mid-May–mid-October, 8:30 A.M.–4:30 P.M. Mon.–Fri. mid-Oct.–mid-May, $3.90 adults, $3.40 seniors over 65, $1.90 children 6–16) from where you can see most of the town and far out over the wild North Atlantic Ocean. Signal Hill, which is now a national historic site, was given its name more than 300 years ago when flags were flown from it to alert townspeople of

approaching ships—letting them know if they were friends or enemies. It also made history when the famous Italian inventor Guglielmo Marconi stood on its summit to receive the very first transatlantic radio signal in 1901. (The kite he used to hold his long aerial aloft in the wind is on display at the Admiralty House Museum in nearby Mount Pearl.)

In addition to the views, the park offers many paths to wander, as well as an excellent geology museum. To get here, take Signal Hill Road (Duckworth Street heading east becomes Signal Hill Road) until you reach the park. The visitors centre is located along Signal Hill Road, across from George's Pond.

Cabot Tower

To get an even better view of the surrounding area, climb the Cabot Tower (9 A.M.–5 P.M. daily mid-April–May, Labour Day–mid-Dec., 8:30 A.M.–9 P.M. daily June–Labour Day, closed mid-Dec.–mid-Apr.), which was built near the crest of Signal Hill in 1897 to commemorate

© PAUL PIGOTT

Cabot Tower

the European discovery of Newfoundland by John Cabot. Today it houses a gift shop and several historic exhibits.

🄲 Johnson Geo Centre and Geo Park

Located at the entrance to the Signal Hill National Historic Park, the Geo Centre (175 Signal Hill Road, 709/724-7625 or 866/868-7625, www.geocentre.ca, 9:30 A.M.–5 P.M. Mon.–Sat., noon–5 P.M. Sun., closed Mon. Oct.–May, $11.50 adults, $9 seniors and students, $5.50 children 5–17) is a mecca for rock hounds as it opens a window onto some of the most ancient geological strata on the planet—the rocks of Signal Hill being 450-million years older than the Rocky Mountains. The centre also features displays about the past and future of the solar system and the evolution of human beings. One exhibit is devoted to the sinking of the *Titanic,* whose distress signal was received nearby. Two theatres show informational films, and the surrounding Geo Park offers a couple of kilometers of looped walkways past traditional stoneworks.

The Battery

A neighborhood perched over the Narrows on the steep cliffs below Signal Hill, the Battery got its name from the military guns that have been placed there and across the channel for hundreds of years to keep enemy ships out of the harbour. Today the residents are still known for sticking up for themselves and for fighting to keep their neighborhood's unique appearance and charm intact. The Battery's narrow winding streets are best approached on foot from the northern end of Water Street, or if by car (slowly, if you please) down from Signal Hill Road. The neighborhood is always open, but of course all the houses are private residences.

🄲 QUIDI VIDI VILLAGE

Found on Quidi Vidi Gut below Quidi Vidi Lake a few minutes north of downtown, this St. John's neighborhood will take you back in time—it retains the rustic look of a 300-year-old fishing village. A visit to an antique store here seems fitting, and **Mallard Cottage Antiques and Collectibles** (2 Barrows Road, 709/576-2266) is a wonderfully stuffed shop located within a cottage dating from the 18th century. There's also a popular microbrewery here. **Quidi Vidi Brewery** (35 Barrows Road,

709/738-4040, www.quidividibrewery.ca, daily, $10 tour) offers tours and cold beer.

To get to Quidi Vidi, take Forest Road east out of downtown; Forest Road turns into Quidi Vidi Village Road.

DOWNTOWN
Railway Coastal Museum

Located in the city's unused but restored 1903 Newfoundland Railway Station, the museum (495 Water Street West, 709/724-5929, www.railwaycoastalmuseum.ca, summer 10 A.M.–5 P.M. daily, Oct. 16–May 31 10 A.M.–5 P.M. Tues.–Sat., noon–5 P.M. Sun., closed Mon., $6 adults, $5 seniors and students, $4 children 5–17) was established after the railway was shut down as a way to preserve and display artifacts, documents, and history. It emphasizes the importance of rail transportation and the coastal boat services to Newfoundland and Labrador's culture. It features pictorial exhibits and dioramas, models of famous ships and trains, and an original 1927 REO Speedwagon delivery truck. A short walk south of the St. John's Harbour, the museum grounds are the location of Mile Zero of the Newfoundland T'Railway and the TransCanada Trail.

◖ The Rooms

The Rooms (9 Bonaventure Avenue, 709/757-8000, www.therooms.ca, 10 A.M.–5 P.M. Mon.–Sat., until 9 P.M. Wed., noon–5 P.M. Sun., archives closed Sun., adults $7.50, seniors and students $5, youth $4, free 6–9 P.M. Wed. and first Sat. of the month) house the **Provincial Museum, the Provincial Art Gallery,** and the **Provincial Archives** in a landmark building, constructed at the crest of the harbour hills upon the ruins of the 250-year-old Fort Townsend. All sections are open to the public, each with exhibits to view and reference materials to consult. As an expression of the purpose of The Rooms, the high, sharp rooflines of the three large wings are meant to mimic and commemorate the old harbourside fishing "rooms" that fishermen and their families used for hundreds of years throughout Newfoundland to process and store their ocean harvests.

The Provincial Museum focuses on the land and people of Newfoundland and Labrador. In one of the permanent exhibits, the foundations of the old Fort Townsend have been uncovered and put on display in the basement of the museum.

The Provincial Art Gallery has exhibits on view from its permanent collection, as well as temporary shows. The archives holds provincial government records, as well as other historical documents relevant to Newfoundland and Labrador, and its exhibits focus on the history of the province.

Bannerman Park

This park has a history that dates back to the 1800s and is a spot close to downtown (albeit up a hill) with wide grassy areas. It's also home to the **Colonial Building,** a massive neoclassical structure that is undergoing renovation until 2013. Built in the early 1850s to house the Newfoundland Legislature, the Colonial Building is constructed with white limestone, all of which was imported from Ireland. The site has been a quiet place since the government moved to the Confederation Building in 1959, but the grounds used to see a lot of excitement, often in the form of riots, when they were at the heart of Newfoundland's political life. Nearby is another historic building, the sandstone **Government House,** where the lieutenant governor of Newfoundland and Labrador lives.

To get to Bannerman Park, follow Military Road around the hill to Bannerman Road.

C. A. PIPPY PARK

At over 1,200 hectares (that's around 3,400 acres) in size, Pippy Park (www.pippypark.com) can boast of being one of the largest urban greenspaces in Canada. Since it is so close to many of the city's residential areas, it has become a popular place to hike in the summer and cross-country ski during the winter. The park contains two golf courses, a campground, as well as the sights like the Fluvarium and the Memorial University Botanical Garden.

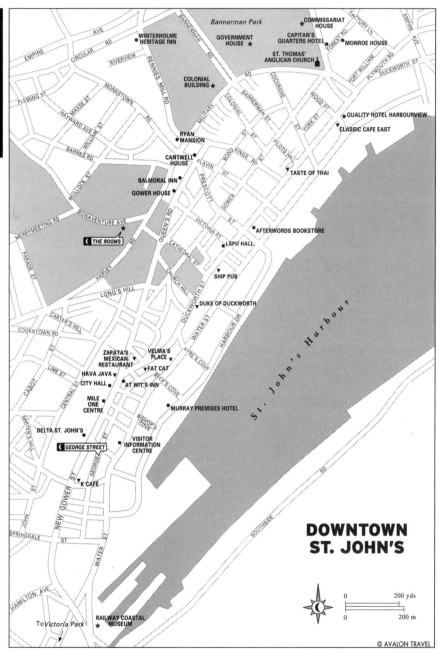

DOWNTOWN ST. JOHN'S

St. John's Harbour

Bannerman Park

COMMISSARIAT HOUSE
WINTERHOLME HERITAGE INN
GOVERNMENT HOUSE ★
CAPITAN'S QUARTERS HOTEL
MONROE HOUSE
ST. THOMAS' ANGLICAN CHURCH
COLONIAL BUILDING ★
QUALITY HOTEL HARBOURVIEW
CLASSIC CAFE EAST
RYAN MANSION
CANTWELL HOUSE
TASTE OF THAI
BALMORAL INN
GOWER HOUSE
AFTERWORDS BOOKSTORE
THE ROOMS
LSPU HALL
SHIP PUB
DUKE OF DUCKWORTH
ZAPATA'S MEXICAN RESTAURANT
VELMA'S PLACE
FAT CAT
HAVA JAVA
CITY HALL
AT WIT'S INN
MILE ONE CENTRE
MURRAY PREMISES HOTEL
DELTA ST. JOHN'S
VISITOR INFORMATION CENTRE
GEORGE STREET
K CAFE
RAILWAY COASTAL MUSEUM
To Victoria Park

0   200 yds
0   200 m

© AVALON TRAVEL

Fluvarium

Built within Pippy Park, the Fluvarium (5 Nagle Place, 709/754-3474, www.fluvarium.ca, summer 9 A.M.–5 P.M. Mon.–Fri., 10 A.M.–5 P.M. Sat. and Sun., Sept.–Jun. 9 A.M.–4:30 P.M. Mon.–Fri., noon–5 P.M. Sat. and Sun., $7 adults, $5 seniors and students, $4 children under 14) features a panoramic window that looks into an otherwise seldom-seen underwater world, revealing life below the surface of the Rennie's River, a freshwater habitat for eels, frogs, trout, arctic char, and salmon. (You won't find the word "fluvarium" in the dictionary: It's a play on "aquarium," using the Latin root for river, "fluv.") The Fluvarium also offers scientific displays, a gift shop, nature trails, conference services, and an outdoor cafe that opens in the summer months. Otherwise, the facility is open year-round, although with reduced hours in the off-season.

Memorial University Botanical Garden

This botanical garden (306 Mount Scio Road, 709/864-8590, www.mun.ca/botgarden, 10 A.M.–5 P.M. daily May–Sept., 10 A.M.–4 P.M. daily Oct.–Nov., 8:30 A.M.–4 P.M. Mon.–Fri. Dec.–Apr., $6 adults, $4 seniors, $2.50 children 6–18, discounted admission during low-season months) features flower gardens and walking paths in its mission to educate and to help students and visitors alike appreciate the plants of Newfoundland and Labrador. Among the blooming patches, there is a medicinal garden, a Newfoundland heritage garden, and others. Nature trails weave through the park and take visitors through different botanical environments, such as boreal forest and Newfoundland barrens. A gift shop and cafe are located in the Field Centre at the entrance to the gardens.

GREATER ST. JOHN'S
Victoria Park

Established to commemorate Queen Victoria in the 1800s, Victoria Park is one of the smallest parks in the city, but also one of the most peaceful and beautiful. The grassy terraces are home to a forest of mature trees and also to several sports facilities, including a ball field and an outdoor swimming pool. Located just south of downtown, the park descends alongside Alexander Street from Hamilton Avenue to Waterford Bridge Road.

Munday Pond Park

This is one of the city's newest parks, and most of it was built only recently on reclaimed land around the rehabilitated Munday Pond, which now attracts migrating ducks and geese in the spring and fall. The trail that circles the pond for a little more than a kilometer is a favorite for joggers and walkers and a good place to see the pond's wildlife. There is also a modern and popular baseball field at the south end of the park. Munday Pond Park is located in a residential neighborhood a few kilometers west of downtown and is accessed via a large unpaved parking lot at the corner of Munday Pond Road and Pearce Avenue. A large unpaved parking lot is located at the corner of Munday Pond Road and Pearce Avenue.

Bowring Park

Found south of downtown St. John's up the Waterford River valley, Bowring Park, with its wide lawns set amidst rushing streams and shady woods, is a favorite place for picnics, strolling, jogging, or just hanging around in the warm sun. There is also a baseball field and an outdoor swimming pool open to the public in the summer months. Bowring Park lies about four kilometers south of the harbour and can be reached by following the paved bike and walking trail up the Waterford River, or by driving up the Waterford Bridge Road to one of several well-marked parking lots.

Cape Spear National Historic Site

Within sight of Signal Hill, but still an 11-kilometer drive from downtown St. John's, rugged, windswept Cape Spear (Route 11/Cape Spear

Drive, 709/772-5367, www.pc.gc.ca, visitors centre 8:30 A.M.–9 P.M. daily mid-May–Labour Day, 10 A.M.–6 P.M. daily Labour Day–mid-Oct., $3.90 adults, $3.40 seniors over 65, $1.90 children 6–16) forms the easternmost point of the North American continent—not counting Greenland. Stand on the rocks looking out to sea and there's nothing between you and Ireland but water. In fact, you'll be closer to London, England, than to Vancouver, British Columbia. The operational **lighthouse** (10 A.M.–6 P.M. daily mid-May–mid-Oct.) now on the site was built in the 1950s, replacing the function of the original, but obsolete, 1835 station, which has since been restored and maintained as an historic artifact. Cape Spear is also the site of a Second World War coastal gun battery and several walking trails.

Admiralty House Museum and Archives

Learn the secrets that only the spies knew—visit a museum (23 Old Placentia Road, Mount Pearl, 709/748-1124, www.admiraltymuseum.ca, 10 A.M.–4 P.M. Mon.–Fri., $3) that was originally built by the Marconi Telegraph Company at the start of the First World War for the Royal Navy to intercept enemy naval transmissions. Today the quarters built for the station officers in 1916 are maintained as an exhibit. Also, and most notably, the museum houses the original kite Guglielmo Marconi flew to receive the first transatlantic wireless signal in 1901. The museum is open and stages special events throughout the year. A little out of the way, it's located in Mount Pearl—the Twin City of St. John's—but it's worth the trip.

Sports and Recreation

HIKING

The **Grand Concourse Authority** (www.grandconcourse.ca, 709/737-1077) maintains around 125 kilometers of walking and biking trails throughout St. John's, connecting almost every park and greenspace to the downtown areas of the city. Their website includes time estimates, length, and a map showing the path for each of their trails.

Signal Hill

Several footpaths, generally a kilometer or two in length, lead from the Signal Hill National Historic Site to various other destinations of equal interest. The following two trails start at the parking lot at the top of the hill. The 1.7-kilometer **North Head Walking Trail** leads down toward a view eastward off North Head and then swings back to an old cliff-side neighborhood called the Outer Battery. Though popular, the North Head Trail features steep sections and is strenuous. The **Ladies Lookout Trail** heads north to meet the **Cuckold Cove Trail,** which, if taken to the left, leads to the Johnson Geo Centre and Geo Park and, if

taken to the right, comes out at Quidi Vidi Village.

C. A. Pippy Park

Access to more than a dozen kilometers of trails for hiking (and skiing in the winter) can be gained from numerous locations within Pippy Park (www.pippypark.com), including at the very end of Allandale Road (where space to park is limited to the dirt shoulder), from the large paved parking lots off the Confederation Building on Prince Philip Drive, and off the Grand Concourse Walk up the Rennie's River Trail from Quidi Vidi Lake. The Grand Concourse Authority maintains a number of trails within Pippy Park, such as the 2.8 kilometer Long Pond Walk.

BOAT TOURS

The waters around St. John's are home to puffins, humpback whales, and icebergs, making some of the city's memorable sights only accessible by boat. Two operators on St. John's Harbour offer boat tours, both leaving from Pier 7 on Harbour Drive, although neither company guarantees any sightings.

Dee Jay Charter Boat Tours (Pier 7, 709/753-8687 on season or 709/726-2141 off season, www.deejaycharters.ca, $40 adults, $20 children under 16) is the more established of the two. The MV *Shanadithi II*—named after the last of Newfoundland's Beothic people—takes passengers from St. John's Harbour out through the Narrows, around into Quidi Vidi Gut, and then south again to Freshwater Bay, Blackwater Bay, and Cape Spear. The tours last 2.5 hours and start three times a day during the summer: 10 A.M., 2 P.M., and 6 P.M. Private charters (three hours, $800) can include a tour of the Quidi Vidi Brewery if the passengers wish.

Iceberg Quest Ocean Tours (Pier 7, 135 Harbour Drive, 866/720-1888, www.iceberg-quest.com, $55 adults, $25 children under 12) offers more frequent but shorter trips, passing through the Narrows to head straight south to Cape Spear and back again in two hours. Iceberg Quest has daily departures during the summer at 9:30 A.M., 1 P.M., 4 P.M., and 7 P.M. Private charters are also available.

The town of Bay Bulls, a 25-minute drive south of St. John's, is also a popular launching point for boat tours to see whales and puffins, with some companies more confident that you'll have a sighting of some sort. Many outfitters in Bay Bulls can also arrange transportation from St. John's.

GOLF

Pippy Park (709/753-7110, www.pippypark. com) has two golf courses: **Captain's Hill** (9-hole) and **Admiral's Green** (18-hole), which includes a clubhouse. Both can be reached off Allandale Road.

Entertainment and Events

NIGHTLIFE

Many of the city's most popular drinking establishments and live music venues are located along the half-kilometer-long George Street that runs parallel to Water Street near the south end of the harbour. However, as famous as George Street is among residents and visitors alike, it is by far not the only place to go in the city for a drink or to listen to some music.

Pubs

For the **Ship Pub** (Solomon's Lane, 709/753-3870, $5–25 cover), which was until recently called the Ship Inn, a name change (made by new owners to avoid confusing anyone seeking a night's lodging, since none is on offer) has not altered the bar's unofficial status as the city's after-hours cultural headquarters. The Ship is found a few flights down the stairway called Solomon's Lane that descends from Duckworth Street (across from the Fraize Law Offices at 268 Duckworth) down to Water Street (across from Asian Variety at 140 Water). The Ship offers a fine selection of liquors, wines, and local beers, and it has acts on stage every week and sometimes every night. The music ranges from East Coast traditional and contemporary to reggae, punk, jazz and the blues. Pub food is also served.

Two blocks south of Solomon's Lane is another pub with as good a beer selection (several of which are brewed on site) and even better food, **The Duke of Duckworth** (325 Duckworth Street, 709/739-6344, www.duke-ofduckworth.webs.com, noon–1 A.M. Sun.–Thurs., noon–3 A.M. Fri. and Sat., food served until 8 P.M.) found at the top of Mcmurdo's Lane (another of the downtown St. John's street stairways). Musical acts are less varied—you won't find Irish folk tunes in this Irish pub, but you'll be able to enjoy pop music and monthly jazz sessions.

◖ George Street

The two-block George Street—closed to all but pedestrian traffic outside of daytime business hours—has more bars and nightclubs per square foot than any other street in North

America. Located right off Water Street and close to City Hall, this famous (or infamous) epicenter for nightlife provides an embarrassment of choice and to some perhaps an embarrassment to the senses. There are at least 20 bars to be sampled (there are new ones opening and closing all the time), enough to satisfy almost any taste.

The **Fat Cat** (14 George St., 709/739-5554, www.fatcatbluesbar.com, Tues. and Wed. 8 P.M.–2 A.M., Thurs.–Sat. 8 P.M.–3 A.M.) offers blues, as well as other types of music, while **The Rock House** (8 George Street, 709/579-6832) turns up hard-driving tunes.

Traditional Irish music can be heard at several establishments, but to experience the true George Street spirit you should at least visit **Trapper John's Museum N' Pub** (2 George Street, 709/579-9630, www.trapperjohns.com). Or, try the **Sundance Bar and Grill** (30 George Street, 709/753-7822, http://partyongeorge.ca) for its dance floor and patio.

PERFORMING ARTS
LSPU Hall

Built as a meeting place by the Sons of Temperance after the Great Fire of 1892 destroyed most of the city's downtown, the hall (3 Victoria Street, www.rca.nf.ca, box office noon–5 P.M. Tues.–Fri. and one hour before showtime on performance nights, tickets $10–50 and up) was purchased by the Longshoremen's Protective Union in 1912. (Union officials liked the location because it gave them a view towards Signal Hill where they could see the flags announcing the arrival of ships to the harbour.) Still called the LSPU Hall, the structure was converted into a performing arts space after the Resource Council for the Arts purchased it in 1976. There's something happening almost every day in the newly renovated 198-seat theater, and its stage hosts dozens of high profile shows every year, including plays, musicians, comedy acts, and film festivals.

St. John's Arts and Culture Centre

Although located a good way from downtown in Pippy Park, this 1,007-seat theatre (Pippy Park, corner of Prince Philip Drive and Allandale Road, 709/729-3900, box office noon–6 P.M. Mon.–Sat. or from noon to a half-hour after curtain time on performance days) is well worth the trip for the quality of the performances—as the 100,000 people who fill the seats every year would attest. The center mounts shows and events by, among others, the Newfoundland Symphony Orchestra, Just for Laughs Comedy Tour, Open Theatre Company, St. John's International Women's Film Festival, and numerous contemporary musicians.

Mile One Centre

Located right downtown beside City Hall, the Mile One Centre (50 New Gower Street, www.mileonecentre.com, box office noon–5 P.M. daily)—named for being at the eastern end of the TransCanada Highway—can seat 6,250 people for a hockey game and a couple of thousand more for a rock concert. Shows are rare, however, and games even rarer. Often there are only one or two one-night musical acts per month and some months pass without the stadium being used at all. Things pick up a bit in spring and summer, first with provincial hockey play-offs and later with the addition of industry shows, festivals, and roller skating.

FESTIVALS
Summer

The **Newfoundland Screech Comedy Festival** (709/579-3378, www.newscreechcomedyfest.com) is on stage at the Holy Heart Theatre (55 Bonaventure Ave., 709/579-4424, www.holyhearttheatre.com) for about a week in early June and features comedic shows as well as stand-up acts.

For lovers of music, the unique **Sound Symposium** (709/753-4630, www.soundsymposium.com) held in early July on even-numbered years, takes place city-wide and features a range of musical art, such as a medley of tunes played by the horns of ships in the harbour.

The **Wreckhouse International Jazz and Blues Festival** (709/739-7734, www.wreckhousejazzandblues.com) is held on 15 different

© PAUL PIGOTT

Spectators gather beside Quidi Vidi Lake to watch the annual Royal St. John's Regatta.

stages all around the downtown for a week in mid-July. In addition to jazz and blues concerts, this festival also features world music.

The **George Street Festival** (709/722-7634, www.georgestreetlive.ca) brings even more of a party to this party street, with six days of band performances in late July.

The oldest organized sporting event in North America, the annual **Royal St. John's Regatta** (www.stjohnsregatta.org) is held on the first Wednesday of August in Quidi Vidi Lake. Rowing teams come from all over the city and the surrounding area to compete against each other in front of large enthusiastic crowds. Regatta Day is the most popular municipal holiday in St. John's.

Also in early August, the **Newfoundland and Labrador Folk Festival** (www.nlfolkfestival.com) comes to Bannerman Park for three days to celebrate the arts and traditions of the province with music and dance.

The **Tuckamore Chamber Music Festival** (709/737-2372, www.tuckamorefestival.

ca) also held in August, with performances spanning two weeks.

One of the more eclectic festivals is the **St. John's Downtown Buskers Festival** (http://downtownstjohns.com), which takes place over three days in early August.

Fall and Winter

Film lovers can go to the various theaters around town to attend the **St. John's International Women's Film and Video Festival** (709/754-3141 or 866/320-7060 www.womensfilmfestival.com) in late October to see the work of women making films from around the world.

Also for film lovers, the **Nickel Independent Film Festival** (709/576-3378, http://nickelfestival.com) is held in mid-December to provide a screen for local, Canadian, and some international films.

The **St. John's Storytelling Festival** (www.storytellingstjohns.ca) is held at various venues in both St. John's and Mount Pearl, usually in early November.

Shopping

ARTS AND CRAFTS

The artists and craftspeople of Newfoundland and Labrador are justifiably famous for the beauty and quality of their work, much of which can be seen and purchased at various places in St. John's. For example, the **Richard Steele Gallery** (63 Harvey Road, 709/754-6741, www.richardsteele.com) offers local heritage fine art, including watercolours and acrylic paintings.

The **Art and Frame Shoppe** (30 Kenmount Road, http://newfoundlandart.net, 709/738-0360 or 877/709-0360) in the Avalon Mall parking lot has the works of more than two dozen local contemporary artists on display for sale.

The **Devon House Craft Centre** (59 Duckworth Street, 709/753-2749) across from the Fairmount Newfoundland sells both traditional and contemporary works in stone, bone, clay, wood, cloth, metal and glass.

ANTIQUES

Shop for antiques inside an antique building: **Mallard Cottage Antiques and Collectibles** (2 Barrows Road, 709/576-2266) in Quidi Vidi Village occupies a cottage dating from the 18th century.

BOOKSTORES

St. John's has suffered the same loss of independent bookshops as other Canadian cities, but enough survive to provide some variety. There is an outlet of the nation-wide **Chapters** (70 Kenmount Road, 709/726-0375, www.chapters.indigo.ca) chain. More adventurous readers can find the **Afterwords Book Store** (221 Duckworth Street, 709/753-4690).

The **Bookery on Signal Hill** (42 Powers Court, 709/739-4223) occupies a heritage home from 1804 and features antique clocks in addition to books.

Accommodations

St. John's is not an inexpensive place to spend the night, or a week, but there are plenty of accommodations available downtown or further afield to meet almost any budget.

DOWNTOWN

For those seeking a comfortable room at the low end of the price range, or for someone who simply prefers small cozy inns to large hotels, there are a good number of reasonably priced bed-and-breakfasts clustered around downtown—most of them established in restored heritage homes.

The four-room **At Wit's Inn** (3 Gower Street, 709/739-7420, www.atwitsinn.ca, $79–129) is fashioned in the Victorian style. Most rooms have one queen bed, and one room has two singles.

The **Gower House** (180 Gower Street, 709/754-0058, $39–229) offers three cozy rooms in a historic townhouse.

The four-room **Balmoral House** (38 Queen's Road, 709/754-5721 or 877/428-1055, www.balmoralhouse.com, $99–169) offers comfortable accommodations, which include breakfast, and the rooms in front have good views.

The three-room **Cantwell House** (25 Queen's Road, 709/754-8439, www.cantwellhouse.nf.net, $65–110) is also done up with Victorian touches, and each room has a fireplace.

One unique yet inexpensive place to stay is the historic **Captain's Quarters Hotel** (2 King's Bridge Road, 709/576-7173, www.captainsquarters.ca, $79–179). The old hotel offers comfortable rooms in an antique building, free breakfast, a cozy in-house bar, and a dining patio on the shady front yard.

Among the mid-range hotels, the most sumptuous is the 11-room **Winterholme Heritage**

Inn (79 Rennie's Mill Road, 709/739-7979 or 800/599-7829, www.winterholme.com, $139–229), located across from Bannerman Park. The Winterholme, a National Historic Site built in the Queen Anne revival style in 1905, offers luxury accommodations and an in-house spa.

Close to downtown is the 160-room **Quality Hotel Harbourview** (2 Hill O'Chips, 709/754-7788, www.qualityinn.com, $109–199), featuring standard chain-hotel accommodations in a central location.

The 47-room **Murray Premises Hotel** (5 Beck's Cove, 709/738-7773, www.murray-premiseshotel.com, $139–349) operates on the boutique concept: higher-end features in a small, quirky property. In this case, the building dates from before the Great Fire in 1892.

The **Delta St. John's** (120 New Gower Street, 709/739-6404, www.deltahotels.com, $99–750) is massive compared to many accommodations options in St. John's. Its 403 rooms come with either a king bed or two doubles, and larger suites are available.

Downtown inns that start in a higher range are less common. The **Ryan Mansion** (21 Rennie's Mill Road, www.ryanmansion.com, 709/753-7926, $185–485) is a boutique hotel located near Bannerman Park. Rooms offer such luxuries as Frette linens and heated bathroom floors.

The seven-room **Monroe House** (8 Forest Road, 709/754-0610, www.monroehouse.nf.ca, $225–450) is a high-end bed-and-breakfast, furnished in a wood-and-brocade style.

OUTSIDE DOWNTOWN

Beyond the St. John's downtown core along the waterfront, hotels are less numerous, but there's an equal range of selection.

The **Travelers Inn** (199 Kenmount Road, 709/722-5540, www.travellersinnstjohns.com, $89–149) offers standard rooms with a bit of a corporate feel, but the property is pet friendly.

The **Guv'nor Inn** (389 Elizabeth Avenue, 709/726-0092, www.guvnor-inn.com, $99–199) is located out toward Pippy Park, and the rooms come with the usual accommodations. There's also a pub in the building, serving up grub like fish-and-chips and other hearty favorites.

For those in the mood for some holistic pampering during their visit, there's the **Spa at the Monastery and Suites** (63 Patrick Street, 709/754-5800, www.monastery-spa.com, $100–250). You can stay in one of the 25 rooms, which each come with an air-massage tub, among other amenities, or just book a treatment at the spa.

In Mount Pearl, the Twin City of St. John's, the **Greenwood Lodge and Motel** (53 Greenwood Crescent, Mount Pearl, 709/364-5300, www.greenwood.nfol.ca, $65–85) has 20 basic rooms, as well as a separate cabin, to offer. It's a lower-priced alternative to staying in town.

CAMPGROUNDS

The **Pippy Park Campground** (709/737-3669, www.pippypark.com, $20 tent sites, $27–42 other sites) has 216 serviced and unserviced lots that accommodate tents, RVs, and camping trailers. The campground is located opposite the Fluvarium on Nagle's Place.

Food

DOWNTOWN

For a good cup of coffee and a snack, **Hava Java** (258 Water Street, 7:30 A.M.–11 P.M. Mon.–Thurs., 8 A.M.–11:30 P.M. Fri. and Sat., 7:30 A.M.–11 P.M. Sun.) will definitely fit the bill with a relaxed, but cultured atmosphere and excellent fare.

For breakfast any time of the day, an excellent place to start is the **K Café** (155 New Gower Street, 709/754-2266, www.k-cafe.ca, 7 A.M.–11 P.M. Sun.–Thurs., 7 A.M.–midnight Fri. and Sat., $13–25 dinner). K Café also serves a hearty menu of seafood and chicken for lunch and dinner.

Lunch can be found at **Velma's Place** (264

Water Street, 709/576-2264, 8:30 A.M.–10 P.M. Mon.–Sat., 9 A.M.–10 P.M. Sun.), which offers traditional Newfoundland cuisine like toutons, fish cakes and seafood chowder.

The **Classic Cafe East** (73 Duckworth Street, 709/726-4444, http://classicca-feeast.com, 8 A.M.–10 P.M. daily summer, 8 A.M.–9 P.M. daily off-season, $14–22 evening menu) serves lunch and a decent supper from a reasonably priced menu that includes steak, pork, and all kinds of seafood.

For less common but still good fare, try **Zapata's Mexican Restaurant** (8–10 Bate's Hill, 709/576-6399, www.zapatas.ca, noon–2 P.M., 4:30–10:30 P.M. Mon.–Thurs., noon–2 P.M., 4:30 P.M.–midnight Fri., 4:30 P.M.–midnight Sat., 4:30–10:30 P.M. Sun. $15–20 dinner), which serves Mexican food classics like burritos and enchiladas.

For the flavors of another continent, the **Taste of Thai** (179 Duckworth Street, 709/738-3203, www.tasteofthainl.com, noon–3 P.M., 5 P.M.–close daily, $14–17) serves up curries, noodles, and some vegan options for lunch and dinner.

OUTSIDE DOWNTOWN
Papa's Pier 17 (15 Rowan Street, 709/753-7692), by Churchill Square near near Memorial University and Pippy Park, has a vaguely Greek focus, but also serves a range of other meat and pasta dishes.

Information and Services

TOURIST INFORMATION
The city's **Visitor Information Centre** (348 Water Street, 709/576-8106, 9 A.M.–4:30 P.M. Mon.–Fri., 9 A.M.–5 P.M. Sat. and Sun.) is located downtown.

MEDIA AND COMMUNICATIONS
Newpapers
St. John's is served by one daily newspaper, *The Telegram,* and by a monthly called *The Scope,* which deals mostly with cultural affairs and the arts.

Television and Radio
Two television stations broadcast from the city, CBC and NTV, as well as several radio stations including VOAR 120 FM and OZ-FM, The Rock of the Rock.

Post Office
Canada Post (354 Water Street, 866/607-6301, www.canadapost.ca, 8 A.M.–5 P.M. Mon.–Fri.) has its main retail location downtown, but other outlets have been established in various pharmacies around the city.

HEALTH AND SAFETY
St. John's is policed by the **Royal Newfoundland Constabulary** (1 Fort Townsend, 709/729-8000) from their headquarters near The Rooms. The RNC can be reached in the case of emergency by dialing 911.

Health matters can be seen to at the **St. Clare's Mercy Hospital** (154 LeMarchant Road, 709/777-5000) or at the **St. John's Health Sciences Centre** (300 Prince Philip Drive, 709/777-6300).

Getting There and Around

GETTING THERE
By Air
The **St. John's International Airport** (80 Airport Terminal Access Road, 709/758-8500 or 866/758-8581, www.stjohnsairport.com) has direct flights coming from all over North America and parts of Europe and is served by six airlines, including Air Canada, WestJet, and United. It is located less than six kilometers northwest of downtown. Although there is no public bus route that serves the airport, taxi service is available—the trip to or from downtown will cost about $30.

By Bus
DRL Coachlines (888/263-1854, www.drl-lr.com) is the only company that offers a daily bus service to and from St. John's, with two terminals in the city: **Memorial University Centre** (off Prince Philip Drive) and the **Crossroads Motel** (980 Kenmount Road, 709/368-3191). The bus leaves the Memorial University Centre stop at 7:30 A.M. every morning and takes almost 14 hours to cross the island of Newfoundland, ending its journey at the Marine Atlantic ferry terminal in Port aux Basques in southwest Newfoundland.

GETTING AROUND
By Bus
Metrobus Transit (709/722-9400, www.metrobus.com) serves most of St. John's (but not the St. John's International Airport) with 18 routes that run 6 A.M.–12:20 A.M. Monday-Saturday and 8 A.M.–8:30 P.M. Sunday. Regular fare costs $2.25 adults and $1.75 children.

By Car
If you need to rent a car, there are six rental companies at St. John's International Airport: Avis, Budget, Hertz, Enterprise, National, and Thrifty. Driving around St. John's is fairly simple, once you get used to the steep hills, the frequent one-way streets, and the almost total lack of city planning. Keep in mind that finding a parking spot anywhere downtown on a busy night is close to impossible.

Avalon Peninsula

BAY BULLS
The first stop outside the city limits south on Route 10 is the town of Bay Bulls (www.baybulls.com), which is about a 25-minutes away from St. John's by car. The main reason to visit is to get out on the water: You have your choice of whale- and puffin-watching boat tours out to Witless Bay Ecological Reserve.

Witless Bay Ecological Reserve
Located off the coast a few kilometers south of Bay Bulls, the Witless Bay Ecological Reserve is a prime bird-watching destination. Its four islands boast the largest puffin colony in North America, as well as a significant population of Leach's storm petrel and other seabirds. In the interest of protecting these habitats, visitors cannot make landfall on the islands, so to see the reserve, you can take a boat tour. The more adventurous can also kayak the waters around the reserve.

Boat Tours
O'Brien's Whale and Bird Tours (709/753-4850, www.obriensboattours.com) operates frequent trips every day during the peak season in small Zodiacs (12 passengers) and larger 46-foot, 83-passenger boats to see wildlife and natural coastline wonders like towering seastacks, cascading waterfalls, and possibly icebergs. Tour Witless Bay Ecological Reserve (2 hours, $55 adults, $50 seniors, $25

EAST COAST TRAIL

For a real wilderness experience that takes almost no drive at all, the 540-kilometer-long East Coast Trail starts at the very doorstep of the capital. From Quidi Vidi, it heads north to Pouch Cove at the northern tip of the finger of land it shares with St. John's. It also heads south from Fort Amherst (the tiny neighbourhood on the south side of the St. John's Narrows), all the way past dozens of communities and scenic wonders to the historic fishing town of Trepassy at the south end of the peninsula.

The East Coast Trail is made up of a series of 22 old and new footpaths that offer the best – or sometimes the only – way to visit the sites of many lighthouses, abandoned settlements, majestic shorelines, seabird colonies, and ecological reserves. Each section of the trail can be walked in about a day, although they all present differing ranges of difficulties for hikers. Well-marked tent-camping sites have been prepared along most sections of the trail, and hotels or bed-and-breakfasts can be found in most of the communities along the way. For more information and to purchase maps, contact the **East Coast Trail Association** (St. John's, 709/738-4453, www.eastcoasttrail.com).

© PAUL PIGOTT

one of many beautiful, rocky, and dangerous ocean coves that can be reached on foot along the East Coast Trail

children 3–10) on a large boat, or venture out with a smaller group (1.5 hours, $85). The company offers a shuttle service ($25) from several large St. John's hotels for an additional charge.

Gatherall's Puffin and Whale Watch (709/334-2887, www.gatheralls.com, May–late Sept., 1.5 hours, $59 adults, $56 seniors, $12 children 2–8) boasts of holding Newfoundland's whale-sighting record, and the company guarantees that their clients will at least spot some puffins. Gatherall's runs one catamaran to Witless Bay from Bay Bulls throughout the summer months.

Third on the Bay Bulls list is **Mullowney's Puffin and Whale Tours** (709/745-5061, May–Sept., 2–2.5 hours, call for rates), which offers four trips a day to Witless Bay aboard the 75-passenger MV *Mary Vincent*. The company can arrange transportation to Bay Bulls from St. John's.

Accommodations and Food

Most visitors will likely stay in St. John's since Bay Bulls is an easy drive from the capital. For those preferring to stay in a smaller town, there's the **Bread and Cheese Inn** (48A Bread & Cheese Road, 709/334-3994 or 866/245-0112, www.breadandcheeseinn. com, $105–130), a six-room bed-and-breakfast in a 19th-century building. The inn has a resident chef for its Country Café, but if you're not a guest, be sure to make reservations to eat here.

Getting There

Bay Bulls is located roughly 25 kilometers south of downtown St. John's on Route 10.

FERRYLAND

One of the most important communities along the East Coast Trail (and also along Route 10, for those driving the one hour from St. John's) is the old fishing village of Ferryland.

◖ Colony of Avalon

The town of Ferryland began as the Colony of Avalon in 1621 and has the remains of some of the earliest structures in North America preserved and uncovered for viewing and study. At the **Colony of Avalon Interpretation Centre** (709/432-3200 or 877/326-5669, www.colonyofavalon.ca, 10 A.M.–6 P.M. daily late May–early Oct.), visitors are welcome to view recovered artifacts, witness specialists at work in the Conservation Laboratory, and enjoy dramatic reenactments of colonial life. There's also a guided tour of current archaeological digs and three replanted 17th-century gardens outside.

Entertainment and Events

The Southern Shore Folk Arts Council hosts two seasonal events in the summer that celebrate the area's Irish heritage. (Ferryland does lie along the Irish Loop, after all.) The **Summer Dinner Theatre** (709/432-2052, www.ssfac.com, 7 P.M. Tues., Thurs., Fri. late June–early Sept.) mounts a different production every summer that tells a story of Irish settlers in the area.

The **Southern Shore Shamrock Festival** (www.ssfac.com) usually takes place over a late-July weekend and draws many to Ferryland to dance to Irish-inspired music.

Accommodations

For those wanting to stay in Ferryland, the **Ark of Avalon B&B** (Main Road, 709/432-2861, $79) offers four rooms, though with shared bathrooms.

Getting There

Ferryland is a one-hour drive from St. John's,
located roughly 25 kilometers south of downtown St. John's on Route 10.

THE IRISH LOOP

Routes 10 and 90 are called the Irish Loop—so named for the long legacy of Irish settlement in the area—and include Bay Bulls and Ferryland, as well as points south and west.

Mistaken Point Ecological Reserve

The Mistaken Point Ecological Reserve (709/438-1012, parksinfo@gov.nl.ca, www.env.gov.nl.ca) is famous for preserving the remains of animals that lived on the deep ocean floor more than 500-million years ago—a rare prehistoric treasure that attracts scientists and fossil buffs from all over the world. The provincial government has protected the site since 1984, making the removal of any fossils strictly prohibited. Visitors can go into the reserve by foot only—no other form of transportation is permitted. Guided tours are available late May–early October.

At the very southeastern end of the Avalon Peninsula Mistaken Point Ecological Reserve is located off Route 10, but with a diversion down a 16-kilometer unpaved road out of Portugal Cove South, which is about two hours away from St. John's by car.

Cataracts Provincial Park

Lovers of waterfalls can find a couple gorgeous examples at the Cataracts Provincial Park (709/635-4520, www.env.gov.nl.ca/parks, early June–mid-Sept.). No overnight camping is allowed, but the province has built stairs, trails, and boardwalks to let day visitors climb down the steep river gorge past two spectacular cascades.

Though not technically part of the Irish Loop, this park makes for an extension for those already driving. Turn west at Salmonier onto Route 91 (which, drivers be warned, becomes an unpaved road for 22 kilometers just west of the village of Colinet) to reach the park.

CAPE SHORE LOOP

The Cape Shore loop brings travelers down Route 92 along St. Mary's Bay or Route 100 along the Placentia Bay shore.

Placentia

The "Pleasant Place" as the founders called it, the town of Placentia is the old capital of French-controlled Newfoundland. This community of around 4,000 has retained the atmosphere and rural beauty of the more than half-dozen fishing villages that came together to form today's modern and scenic seaside town.

The engineering marvel that is the **Sir Ambrose Shea Lift Bridge** connects Placentia with its northern neighbour Jerseyside. It was built in 1961 to save townspeople from having to cross an often-dangerous channel in small open boats.

The home of the famous Magistrate William O'Reilly is now the **O'Reilly House Museum** (48 Orcan Drive, 709/227-5568, http:// placentia.20m.com). This well-preserved Victorian home displays the furnishings and appointments of the period. In addition to the displays, the museum offers **walking tours** of the town every Tuesday and Thursday at 2 P.M. throughout the summer. Guides dress in 18th-century costume, and they provide a wealth of information about many local sights, historical and otherwise.

Placentia has the **Placentia Bay Cultural Arts Centre** (21 Patterson Dr., 709/227-2787) on the Town Square for musical, comedy, and other special events. The **Placentia Area Theatre D'Heritage** (www.placentiatheatre. ca) does full shows at various venues around town.

For accommodations in the area, try the historic five-room **Rosedale Manor** (40 Orcan Drive, 709/227-3613 or 877/999-3613, www. rosedalemanor.ca). For those looking for a place to park recreational vehicles, the **Argentia Sunset Park** (709/227-6363, June–Oct.) is located less than three kilometers from the Marine Atlantic ferry terminal.

Placentia is a 1.5-hour drive from St. John's

along the TransCanada Highway and Route 100. The ferry terminal for **Marine Atlantic** (800/341-7981, www.marine-atlantic.ca) is in Argentia, just north of Placentia. Ferries connect Argentia with North Sydney, Nova Scotia with a 15-hour crossing.

Castle Hill National Historic Site

A little north of downtown Placentia is the Castle Hill National Historic Site (709/227-2151, www.pc.gc.ca, visitors centre 10 A.M.–6 P.M. Mon.–Fri. mid-May–mid-Oct., $3.90 adults, $3.40 seniors over 65, $1.90 children 6–16), which encompasses the uncovered foundations of three early forts. The French built two on these heights overlooking the sea: first the Vieux Fort and then Fort Louis. Later the British constructed what was called the New Fort. The area still hosts several archaeological digs that are exploring sites dating back to the 1600s and visitors are welcome to view the ongoing work. Castle Hill sits between Argentia and Placentia, six kilometers from Argentia.

◖ Cape St. Mary's Ecological Reserve

The Cape St. Mary's Ecological Reserve (709/277-1666, parksinfo@gov.nl.ca, www.env. gov.nl.ca, park open year-round, Interpretation Center and guided tours May–Oct.) is a destination for anyone interested in the natural world, but especially a choice location for bird watchers. The cliffs and seastacks off the southwest Avalon Peninsula not only support the world's southernmost breeding colony of Northern Gannets (there's at least 25,000 of them), but also thousands of Murres and Black-legged Kittiwakes. Access to sensitive ground is restricted, but a public vantage point provides a spectacular view over many of the nesting sites. (For a musical description of Cape St. Mary's, track down a copy of the song of the same name by folk singer Stan Rogers.)

Cape St. Mary's is less than an hour's drive south of Placentia along Route 100, and then down an access road 15 kilometers east of St. Bride's.

© PAUL PIGOTT

children playing on a Bell Island beach

AROUND CONCEPTION BAY

Conception Bay lies to the west of St. John's, and destinations in and around it make for nice excursions from the capital.

Bell Island

On the eastern shore of Conception Bay, one comes to the town of Portugal Cove, where a frequent ferry makes the short run to Bell Island. A good day trip from St. John's, the island offers quiet woods, pebbly beaches, and panoramic outlooks over the bay, like the one from the **Bell Island Gunsite** (Beach Hill, 709/488-2990), which was manned by Newfoundland Militia during the Second World War to protect the island's only harbour.

Bell Island is mostly known for its century-old abandoned iron ore mines. **Bell Island's Mine Museum and Underground Tour** (1 Compressor Hill, 709/488-2880, www.bellisland.net, 11 A.M.–7 P.M. daily June–Sept., $10 adults, $8 seniors, $3 children 12 and under)

features tours of several of the old shafts, and the museum hosts displays of mining artifacts as well as a superb collection of pictures of local miners taken by world famous photographer Yousuf Karsh.

For people wanting to stay on Bell Island, the eight-room **Belle of the Bay Inn** (82 Memorial Street, Wabana, 709/488-2500, www.belleofthebayinn.ca, $100–150) is a bed-and-breakfast located only a few minutes from the ferry docks. It is housed in a building that was once a convent, and there is also an on-site cafe and bistro.

The ferry (709/535-6244, www.tw.gov.nl.ca, $2.25 adults, $1.75 seniors, $1.75 children) to Bell Island departs Portugal Cove multiple times daily. Portugal Cove is 20 minutes northwest of St. John's by car.

Cupids

North of the TransCanada Highway around Conception Bay is the historic and pretty community of Cupids. In Cupids, visitors can tour the archaeological site of English Canada's first colony, **Cupers Cove** (Seaforest Drive, Cupids, 709/596-1906, www.baccalieudigs.ca, June–Oct.), which was settled 400 years ago, making it the oldest surviving British colony in Canada and second only to the famous Jamestown Settlement in North America.

The **Cupids Museum** (Seaforest Drive, Cupids, 709/528-3500, 10 A.M.–5 P.M. daily mid-June–mid-Oct.) exhibits, among other items, artifacts from the old colony.

Cupids is located approximately 90 kilometers from St. John's, off Route 70 from the TransCanada Highway.

CENTRAL AND WESTERN NEWFOUNDLAND

Central Newfoundland is essentially two spectacular rocky coastlines separated by hundreds of kilometers of uninhabited forest and wilderness reserve. The northern coastline is the easier of the two to reach, since the TransCanada Highway runs across that part of the island. Here, along what's known as Iceberg Alley and the Great Whale Coast, icebergs and whales are a common sight as they float or swim in the waters offshore. The southern coast of central Newfoundland feels more remote, with long stretches of highway occasionally interrupted by protected parks and a chance to learn about Newfoundland's Mi'kmaq people.

The farther west you go, towns in Newfoundland become more spread apart from each other: The island becomes larger, the hills higher, and the woods deeper. The main destination in western Newfoundland, and possibly the entire province, is Gros Morne National Park, a sweeping landscape of coast, fjords, lakes, rivers, and unusual geology.

Beyond the national park, it's well worth the time to explore the Northern Peninsula up to L'Anse aux Meadows, where the Norse landed a thousand years ago. There are also plenty of small museums for those interested in history and heritage in the many communities of western Newfoundland.

PLANNING YOUR TIME

Beyond the Avalon Peninsula, the vastness of the rest of the island of Newfoundland can fill weeks of exploration. Any one town or park, with the primary exception of Gros Morne National Park, may not warrant more than a

© MICHAEL JOHANSEN

HIGHLIGHTS

◖ **Cape Bonavista:** Celebrated as the location where explorer John Cabot made landfall in 1497 to claim Newfoundland for England, Bonavista has today preserved its maritime history and become a center for summer arts (page 34).

◖ **North Atlantic Aviation Museum:** When Gander was built, Newfoundland quickly became an integral part of all transatlantic air travel, military and civilian. The museum shows it all, plus it has an impressive collection of antique aircraft (page 39).

◖ **Fogo Island:** A prime spot on Iceberg Alley and the Great Whale Coast, Fogo has a wealth of history, culture, and scenery to share with visitors (page 44).

◖ **Grand Lake:** The island's largest body of fresh water, Grand Lake offers miles of boating and fishing and is surrounded by three wildlife and ecological reserves (page 49).

◖ **Marble Mountain:** Unquestionably one of the most popular tourist destinations in Newfoundland, Marble Mountain offers first-class alpine skiing in the winter and a record-breaking zip line all through the year (page 50).

◖ **Bonne Bay Fjords:** Just one of the many natural wonders in Gros Morne National Park, these fjords can be admired from a boat, hiking trails, or even your car (page 51).

◖ **Port au Choix:** The home of Maritime Archaic Indians and Dorset Paleo-Eskimo societies thousands of years ago, the town of Port au Choix and the barren point it's built on are now part of a National Historic Site that cele-

brates the area's ancient and modern history (page 57).

◖ **L'Anse aux Meadows:** Many people believed Norse Vikings reached North America more than 1,000 years ago, but no one knew for sure until this settlement was discovered in the 1960s beneath mysterious mounds on the tip of the Northern Peninsula (page 58).

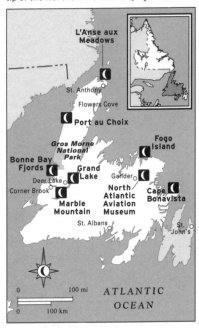

LOOK FOR ◖ TO FIND RECOMMENDED SIGHTS AND ACTIVITIES.

day's visit, but there are many to choose from. Take note of driving distances and the availability of services, as these will affect your trip planning as much as the sightseeing itself.

Driving is the best way to get around; although there is a cross-island DRL Coachline bus that traverses the TransCanada Highway from Port aux Basques to St. John's, the biggest draws are off the TCH. Those not coming

from St. John's can enter from the west by ferry at Port aux Basques or by plane, with main airports in Gander, Deer Lake, and Stephenville.

While the TransCanada Highway is useful for getting from Point A to Point B very quickly, to see all that Newfoundland has to offer, a traveler must leave the TCH and explore the many rural and coastal roads. Some

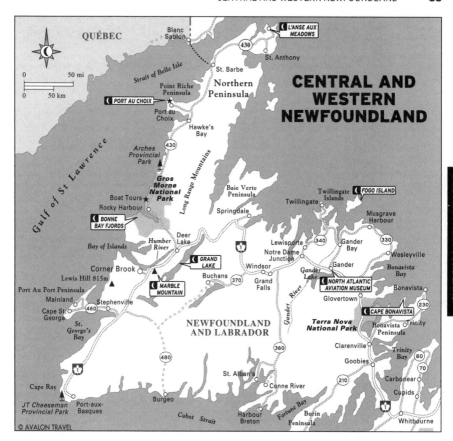

of the secondary highways that branch off the TCH are dead-ends (albeit usually ending at some of the most amazing scenery in the world), but others form loops of various lengths that make convenient and fascinating detours off the main road.

Central and western Newfoundland is a very seasonal destination, with many places, including accommodations, not operational roughly between October and April. (This is not true, of course, of Marble Mountain, a prime skiing destination.) The main travel season is June–August, but iceberg-watchers should keep in mind that the so-called iceberg season is April–July, with May and June the best months to spot them.

Bonavista and Burin Peninsulas

Both the Burin and Bonavista Peninsulas offer many sights worth seeing, but perhaps it's best to start off in the town of Bonavista at the northern end of Route 235.

BONAVISTA

Set on the northern tip of the Bonavista Peninsula, the town of Bonavista is located in a very significant spot in the history of the province.

🕻 Cape Bonavista

Newfoundland history teaches that John Cabot, who discovered the island in 1497, landed at Cape Bonavista to claim the territory for the English Crown. Today the Cape is the site of a lighthouse built in 1841. The **Cape Bonavista Lighthouse Provincial Historic Site** (709/468-7444, 10 A.M.–5:30 P.M. daily, late May–mid-Oct., free on Sundays) is a distinctive red and white structure with historical displays inside. From the cape, you may see whales and puffins off shore.

Other Sights

The town of Bonavista is home to several other features of interest. The **Ryan Premises National Historic Site** (709/468-1600, www. pc.gc.ca, 10 A.M.–6 P.M. daily mid-May–mid-Oct., $3.90 adults, $3.40 seniors over 65, $1.90 children 6–16) is the restored harbourfront property of a 19th-century saltfish merchant. Building 2 now houses the **Bonavista Museum,** which has an interesting collection of artifacts relating to life in the town in the late 1800s.

The 18th century **Mockbeggar Plantation** (Roper Street, 709/468-7300, 10 A.M.–5:30 P.M. daily late May–early Oct., $3 adults, free children under 12) may be the oldest identifiable fishing 'room' still in existence. Here, you can learn about saltfishing, an important industry in the province's history.

A full-sized replica of the *Matthew* (Bonavista Harbour, 877/468-1497, late May–Sept., $7.50

adults, $6.75 seniors, $3 children 6–16, www. matthewlegacy.com), the ship that John Cabot sailed across the Atlantic Ocean in 1497, is on permanent display in the harbour, with tours available in season.

Accommodations and Food

Built as a general store in the 1920s, the **Harbour Quarters Inn** (42 Campbell Street, Bonavista, 709/468-7922 or 866/468-7945, www.harbourquarters.com, $100–235) has 10 rooms and one suite available for people looking for a place to stay in this town. The hotel's **Skipper's Restaurant** (7 A.M.–10 P.M. daily) serves up traditional provincial fare and nice waterfront views.

Getting There

Bonavista is located on Route 230 (and also the northern end of Route 235), roughly 115 kilometers from Clarenville and 300 kilometers (3.5 hours driving) from St. John's.

TRINITY

This little town (www.townoftrinity.com) on Trinity Bay midway along the Bonavista Peninsula preserves its heritage and traditions in its historical buildings. The bay is also an attraction, offering the possibility of seeing whales, birds, and icebergs.

Sights

The Trinity Historical Society runs the **Trinity Museum** (Church Road, 709/464-3599, www. trinityhistoricalsociety.com, mid-May–mid-Oct., $10), which displays items significant to the town's development, such as ice saws and ship tools. The traditional craft of mat hooking is regularly demonstrated, and visitors can give it a try as well.

The oldest wooden church in the province stands in Trinity: the **Church of the Most Holy Trinity** (Ash's Lane at Pie Corner, 709/464-3599, open year-round), built in 1833.

Down the shore, following Route 239 to New Bonaventure, the **Random Passage Site**

(709/464-2209, www.randompassagesite.com, mid-May–mid-Oct., $8 adults, $6 seniors, $3.50 children 6–17) sits as an authentic and accurate replica of a fishing outport of the 1800s built in the year 2000 as a set to film the *Random Passage* television mini-series. During the summer months, musical entertainment is offered on Sundays. New Bonaventure is about 17 kilometers south of Trinity along Route 239.

Boat Tours

Trinity Bay is home base to several tour boat companies that offer the possibility of whale, iceberg, and seabird sightings. **Sea of Whales Adventures** (1 Ash's Lane, 709/464-2200, www.seaofwhales.com, June–Oct., $80 adults, $50 children 3–12) offer three-hour tours of the waters off the Bonavista peninsula, with sightings possible of dolphins, humpback whales, sperm whales, minke whales, as well as, of course, puffins.

You will likely see the usual suspects—whales and seabirds—with **Rugged Beauty Boat Tours** (New Bonaventure, www.ruggedbeautyboattours.net, June–Oct.) in New Bonaventure, but the focus of the three-hour tour is instead on the abandoned communities of the coast, such as Kerley's Harbour. New Bonaventure is about 17 kilometers south of Trinity along Route 239.

In addition to the usual watery attractions also promised by other tour companies, **Trinity Eco-Tours** (10 Main Street, www.trinityecotours.com, $80 adults, $50 children under 12) does guided kayak tours ($59 per person for 2 hours) and also can bring clients (experienced divers only) on recreational dives down to old shipwrecks in nearby waters.

Golf

People who prefer dry land can find some first-class links near Trinity at Princeton, where **The View Golf Resort** (100 Main Street, Princeton, 709/462-8439, www.theviewgolfresort.com, $33 18-hole round) offers nine holes, six tourist suites, and a spacious modern clubhouse, as well, as the name implies, a view over spectacular ocean scenery. Princeton is a 35-kilometer

drive across the Bonavista Peninsula and up Route 235 from Trinity.

Entertainment and Events

For performing arts, try the **Rising Tide Theatre** (Route 239, 709/464-3847, www.risingtidetheatre.com), famous for historical pageants and comedy pieces. Rising Tide also hosts the summertime **Seasons in the Bight Theatre Festival** (mid-June–mid-Oct.)

Accommodations and Food

The nine-room **Bishop White Manor** (Gallavan's Lane, 709/464-3698, $95–160 June–Oct.) is in the former home of the first Anglican bishop born in Newfoundland and exudes a period atmosphere. Breakfast is offered through the next door Eriksen Premises.

The seven-room **Eriksen Premises** (West Street, 709/4646-3327, $95–135 May–Oct.) is in another restored period building. There's also a restaurant connected to the bed-and-breakfast, which serves regional cuisine.

In nearby Port Rexton, just north of Trinity, the **Fisher's Loft Inn** (Mill Road, Port Rexton, 709/464-3240, www.fishersloft.com, $99–250) is set in a traditional outport building. Rooms are decorated with hand-made furniture, and there's also an onsite restaurant.

Getting There

Trinity is roughly 70 kilometers north of Clarenville and 250 kilometers west of St. John's.

CLARENVILLE

Clarenville's claim to fame is being at the western end of the first transatlantic telephone cable. (Oban, Scotland, was at the other.) The town doesn't hold very many tourist sights, but it's located at a key point on the TransCanada Highway for drivers heading toward the Bonavista Peninsula and offers a number of places to sleep.

Entertainment and Events

Clarenville's **Wintertainment** (709/466-7937, www.clarenville.net) hosts snowmobile and

WESTERN NEWFOUNDLAND

tobaggan races, skiing, and snow sculptures for 10 days in February.

Accommodations

The town of Clarenville provides plenty of accommodations, with hotels and bed-and-breakfasts within easy access of the TransCanada Highway.

The 65-room **St. Jude Hotel** (247 TransCanada Highway, 709/466-1717, www.stjudehotel.com, $102–145, suites $145–265) offers standard accommodations right on the TCH.

The 24-room **Restland Motel** (262 Memorial Drive, 709/466-7636, www.restlandmotel.ca, $99–119, suites $130–165) offers basic rooms, as well as suites that include kitchenettes.

South of the TCH, about 15 minutes away from Clarenville, the **Trailside Motel** (Goobies, 709/542-3444, www.trailsidemotel.com, $65–100) rents out 12 simply appointed rooms.

Getting There

Clarenville (www.clarenville.net) is located on the TransCanada Highway, where Route 230 branches off to traverse the Bonavista Peninsula. From St. John's, it's a roughly 180-kilometer, 2-hour drive. Goobies, about 15 minutes south of Clarenville, is the point at which to get off the TCH onto Route 210 to explore the Burin Peninsula.

DRL Coachlines (888/263-1854, www.drl-lr.com), which makes the overland trip from St. John's to Port aux Basques daily, stops at Clarenville Irving in Clarenville and Irving Bigstop at the Goobies Junction.

BURIN PENINSULA

To explore the Burin Peninsula, drivers will need to head down Route 210 from the TransCanada Highway.

Marystown

Down on the Burin Peninsula one of the first places to stop and linger is the community of Marystown, the economic hub of the area. Visitors can find the **Marystown Heritage Museum** (283 Ville Marie Drive, 709/279-2463) to see artifacts from and exhibits about Newfoundland's shipbuilding history.

Those more interested in mini-golf, waterslides, gaming arcades, and long sandy beaches will want to spend some time at the **Golden Sands Amusement Park** (Winterland Road, Marystown, 709/891-2400, $5 per vehicle).

For a place to stay, the 133-room **Marystown Hotel and Convention Centre** (76 Ville Marie Drive, 709/279-1600, www.marystownhotel.com, $109–179) has renovated rooms and free wifi. A restaurant serving seafood and Newfoundland specialties is located here as well.

Marystown is located along Route 210, roughly three hours from St. John's.

The Frenchmans Cove Provincial Park

The Frenchmans Cove Provincial Park (709/635-4520, www.env.gov.nl.ca) offers 51 hectares of beaches and oceanside camping. A protected shoreline habitat for many species of birds, it's also a bird-watching destination. There are 76 campsites, a few with electrical hookups, as well as cabins for rent through a private concessioner. Frenchman's Cove is located on Route 213, 24 kilometers west of Marystown.

Grand Bank

The town of Grand Bank lies on the west side of the Burin Peninsula along Fortune Bay. Like many communities in the area, Grand Bank retains a fishing legacy.

If you happen to be here in the winter, the **Grand Bank Winter Carnival** (709/832-2617, www.townofgrandbank.com) usually runs for a full week starting in late February and features free ice skating, ice sculpting, and snowmobile contests.

Grand Bank also puts on the **Grand Bank Regional Theatre Festival** (709/832-2282, www.grandbankfestival.com) starting the last week of June. Audiences can attend a variety of productions, including dinner theatres and lunchtime plays.

The **Granny's Motor Inn** (33 Grandview Boulevard, 709/832-2180, $84–104, $30 per pet) offers quaint, serviceable rooms for people looking to stay on the Burin Peninsula.

Grand Bank is 30 kilometers south and west of Frenchman's Cove, and the drive from Goobies takes roughly two hours.

Fortune Head Ecological Reserve

Those interested in the outdoors should head west and south of Marystown to the **Fortune Head Ecological Reserve** (709/635-4520, www.env.gov.nl.ca). The Fortune Head Reserve is a good place to view rock strata that is more than 530-million years old.

To get here, drive first to the town of Fortune, which is roughly 210 kilometers down Route 210 from Goobies. From Fortune, take Route 220 about 1.6 kilometers west to reach the reserve.

Lamaline

Lamaline is a town situated on the southern end of Burin Peninsula. The **Lamaline Heritage Museum and Information Centre** (Main St., 709/857-2864, 10 A.M.–5 P.M., Mon.–Sat., July–Sept.) displays more modern exhibits, showing artifacts from the two world wars and from the 1929 tidal wave that devastated many communities on the Burin.

Terra Nova National Park

Terra Nova National Park (www.pc.gc.ca/terranova) is not the largest protected wilderness area in central Newfoundland, but it's the one that's easiest to reach and easiest to use, with the TransCanada Highway running right through it and with plenty of services to offer to visitors. Canada's most easterly national park boasts more than 400 square kilometers of protected forest along almost 200 kilometers of sheltered ocean shoreline.

Orientation

About 40 kilometers of the TransCanada Highway goes right through the park. Approaching from eastern Newfoundland, you will hit **Port Blandford,** a community right outside the eastern entrance to the park, at the junction of the TCH and Route 233. Continuing through the park, the next community is **Charlottetown,** located off the TCH and not technically part of the park, a little over 20 kilometers from Port Blandford. Both towns overlook Clode Sound, one of the Atlantic Ocean's many inlets in this part of Newfoundland.

As you head toward the northern part of the park, the TCH leaves the edge of Clode Sound. **Newman's Sound Campground** is located on Newman's Sound, another inlet, as is the **visitors centre** farther north. The road leading to **Malady Head** is located just inside the western entrance to the park.

SPORTS AND RECREATION

Outdoor recreation is definitely the focus of a trip to Terra Nova National Park.

Hiking

Hikers in the summer and cross-country skiers in the winter have a choice between a number of different trails of varying lengths and difficulties. A map of trails is available in the Hiking section the park website, and a hiking guide is on sale in the gift shop in the visitors centre.

An introductory hike is the three-kilometer/one-hour loop around **Sandy Pond,** where you can get a sense of the forest environment. The road leading to the trail is about half-way between Charlottetown and the Newman Sound Campground.

For experienced hikers, the **Outport Trail** is a 46-kilometer/16-hour hike starting from Newman Sound Campground. It leads to a series of abandoned settlements on Newman Sound, a couple of which have overnight camping spots, and in a bay called the Lions Den.

Also around Newman Sound Campground, about 10 kilometers of trails are kept groomed for skiers throughout the winter.

Boat Tours

Coastal Connections (visitor centre kiosk, Salton's Brook, 709/533-2196, www.coastalconnections.ca, June–Oct., $65 adults, $35 children 17 and under) runs the MV *Coastal Explorer* for 2.5-hour tours of Newman Sound. Leaving from the visitors centre twice a day, the tours can take as many as 12 passengers at a time to explore nearby coastal ecosystems—and also, sometimes, to learn how to fish like a Newfoundlander by drawing crab pots out of the water.

North of the park at Burnside on Route 310, **Burnside Heritage Foundation Archaeological Boat Tours** (709/677-2474, www.burnsideheritage.ca) doesn't just look for icebergs offshore, but also takes passengers to view ancient aboriginal sites, like the millenia-old Bloody Bay Quarry. While these tours don't operate in the park, they can be an excursion for those already in the area.

Kayaking and Boating

Adventure Quest (visitors centre, Salton's Brook, 709/422-1111, www.oceanquestadventures.com, $30 two-hour kayak rental, $40 two-hour canoe rental) rents kayaks and canoes from its location at the visitors centre. Two-hour guided paddles are available for an additional charge.

The park provides a launch site for ocean-going power boats at **Malady Head.**

ENTERTAINMENT AND EVENTS
Festivals

The **Heritage Folk Festival** (www.heritage-foundationtnnp.ca or www.pc.gc.ca/terranova) takes place in Terra Nova National Park for two days toward the end of August and offers traditional musicians from Newfoundland and Ireland. Festivities take place in the Newman Sound day-use grounds.

Outside the park on Route 310, roughly 15 kilometers from the TransCanada Highway, the town of Eastport holds two summer festivals. In mid-July, music lovers can attend **The Beaches Accordion Festival** (709/677-2360, www.beachesheritagecentre.ca) not only to hear a celebration of Newfoundland's favourite musical instrument, but also to take in lots of buskers and a gospel show. In mid-August, the **Winterset in Summer** writing festival brings together provincial literary figures for a three-day weekend of readings, talks, and more.

ACCOMMODATIONS AND CAMPING

Within the park, the only way to spend the night is to camp, but you can find shelter in towns near the park.

Port Blandford

The **Leisure Time Cabins** (709/543-2400, $80 per cabin) are located across from the wharf in Port Blandford and offer rustic two-room cabins.

Terra Nova Cottages (TransCanada Highway, 709/543-2260, www.terranova.nfld.net, $110) offer bed-and-breakfast-style accommodations, with some en-suite rooms, as well as cabins.

Charlottetown

The 20-unit **Clode Sound Motel** (709/664-3146, www.clodesound.com, $70–170), located on the shore of Clode Sound, just a minute from the TransCanada Highway, offers basic rooms, all of which come with a kitchenette. The grounds have a restaurant, picnic areas, and flower gardens.

Campgrounds

The park has two campgrounds (877/737-3783, $20) reachable by car. The larger **Newman Sound Campground** is in the middle of the park and has 100 serviced and 243 unserviced lots. There are a range of facilities available here, including showers and flush toilets, a grocery store (9 A.M.–5 P.M. Sun.–Thurs., 11 A.M.–7 P.M. Fri. and Sat. mid-May–late June,

Labour Day–early Oct., 8 A.M.–10:30 P.M. daily late June–Labour Day), and laundry.

The **Malady Head Campground** (11 A.M.–7 P.M. daily late June–Labour Day) is found at the northern edge of Terra Nova off Route 310 and has 87 unserviced sites. There are showers and flush toilets, but few other amenities.

For backcountry camping, a number of primitive campsites (709/533-2942) that offer tent platforms, fire pits, and nearby pit privies can be found along several wilderness hiking trails.

INFORMATION AND SERVICES
Tourist Information

Also known as the **Marine Interpretation Centre,** the park visitors centre (Salton's Brook, 709/533-2942, www.pc.gc.ca/terranova, 10 A.M.–5 P.M. daily late May–late June, Labour Day–early Oct., 9 A.M.–7 P.M. daily late June–Labour Day) is located in Salton's Brook, roughly 35 kilometers from the park's eastern entrance and 10 kilometers from the park's western entrance. There, you can find exhibits about the park, a gift shop with souvenirs as well as park maps, outfitters for various water activities, and a restaurant.

There is also an administration building (Newman Sound, 709/533-2801, 8:30 A.M.–4:30 P.M. Mon.–Fri.) that is open year-round.

GETTING THERE
By Car

Terra Nova National Park is located, conveniently, along the TransCanada Highway, and its eastern and western entrances are both located along the TCH. The visitors centre is roughly 260 kilometers from St. John's, about a 2.75-hour drive and about 70 kilometers/45 minutes from Clarenville. Approaching from the western part of Newfoundland, Gander is about 75 kilometers away from the visitors centre, about 50-minute drive.

By Bus

DRL Coachlines (888/263-1854, www.drl-lr.com), which makes the overland trip from St. John's to Port aux Basques daily, stops at Blackmore's North Atlantic gas station in Port Blandford.

Gander and Grand Falls-Windsor

GANDER

Gander (www.gandercanada.com) is the prime destination for flying enthusiasts in central Newfoundland. Gander was built just before the Second World War as a stopover for propeller-driven aircraft heading to Europe, and it quickly became important as an airbase for both Canadian and American military forces.

In addition to aviation, Gander may also be famous for its salmon. **Gander River boats** have even been designed to be especially deft in navigating the river's many rapids and pools in the pursuit of these fish. Take note of them while here—the design is unique to this waterway.

◀ North Atlantic Aviation Museum

Gander's aviation history and a collection of planes (including one that appears stuck in the wall above the building entrance) can be seen at the North Atlantic Aviation Museum (TransCanada Highway between the Tourist Chalet and the James Paton Memorial Hospital, 709/256-2923, www.naam.ca, 9 A.M.–6 P.M. daily June–Sept., Mon.–Fri. Oct.–May, $5 adults, $4 seniors and children 5–15). While the actual airplanes might be the main draw, the exhibits inside the museum tell the story of significant incidents in flight in the province.

Other Sights

East of the aviation museum about four kilometers along the TCH overlooking the banks of Gander Lake is the **Silent Witness Memorial** (TransCanada Highway, May 20–Oct. 31,

WESTERN NEWFOUNDLAND

free), built on the site of the 1985 Arrow Air plane crash that took the lives of more than 250 American servicemen.

The **Gander International Airport** (east end of Airport Boulevard, 709/256-6666, www.flygander.ca) itself is something of a living flight museum, but not one that's easy to tour. What is now the secure international departure and arrival hall has escaped renovations and remained essentially unchanged since it was opened by Queen Elizabeth II in 1959. Not only has the furnishings, decor and layout of the original reception area been kept as they were designed more than 50 years ago, but the airport still boasts the original 72-foot mural that depicts humanity's age-old fascination with flight. Curiously, some of the images artist Kenneth Lockhead painted in the 1950s resemble the French Concorde, the famous supersonic passenger jet that wasn't going to be invented for another two decades. Gander Airport's beautiful and fascinating international lounge is no longer open to the general public, but viewings can sometimes be arranged

through the airport's security and administration offices. Definitely make time to appreciate it if you're on a flight into or out of Gander.

Notre Dame Provincial Park

The 133-hectare Notre Dame Provincial Park (709/535-2379, www.env.gov.nl.ca) is on Junction Pond and offers family camping (100 sites) during the summer and cross-country skiing in the winter. With a beach and picnic tables nearby, the park is makes a nice stop on a road trip.

The park is a little over 40 kilometers west of Gander along the TransCanada Highway.

Golf

Serious golfers can find links at the **Gander Golf Club** (251 TransCanada Highway, 709/256-4653, www.gandergolfclub.ca, $47 18 holes). Set next to Gander Lake, the course was designed by Doug Carrick.

Festivals

Gander's **Festival of Flight** (www.gander-canada.com) takes place over the weekend that ends on the first Monday in August. Music, a parade, contests, and, of course, food are all involved in celebrating Gander and aviation. The last day is also **Gander Day Civic Holiday,** which ends with fireworks.

Accommodations and Food

Gander, as a popular destination for business and government travelers, tends to have room prices that are higher than the rest of region.

The Albatross, Hotel Gander, and Sinbad's are all owned by a single company, Steele Hotels. All offer similar, straightforward rooms in a similar price range. **Albatross** (TransCanada Highway, 709/256-3956, www.steelehotels.com, $110) has 90 rooms. There's a seafood restaurant on site, as well as a lounge for drinks.

Sinbad's (Bennett Drive, 709/651-2678, www.steelehotels.com, $110) has a number of suites, making it a good choice for families. There is a surf and turf restaurant on site serving breakfast, lunch, and dinner daily.

© MICHAEL JOHANSEN

Gander River boats on the Gander River

© MICHAEL JOHANSEN

view out the window of a tumbledown fishing shed on the shore of Gander Bay

WESTERN NEWFOUNDLAND

Hotel Gander (100 TransCanada Highway, 709/256-3931, www.hotelgander.com, $130) has 148 rooms on offer in a business-style hotel. There are two restaurants at this hotel: **Tomcats Bar & Grill** has an outdoor sitting area, and you can have lighter fare, while **Alcock & Brown's** serves up dinner in a family atmosphere.

Part of a larger chain, the **Comfort Inn** (112 TransCanada Highway, 709/256-3535, www.comfortinn.com, $150) offers 65 standard rooms.

Getting There

The **Gander International Airport** (east end of Airport Boulevard, 709/256-6666, www. flygander.ca) is not as busy as it was decades ago before fast passenger jets made transatlantic stop-overs largely unnecessary, but it's still used by several airlines, such as Air Canada and Sunwing, that connect the town with destinations within the province, in Canada, and in some Caribbean countries.

Taxi service is available from the airport, and rental car companies Avis, Budget, National, and Thirfty all have kiosks at the terminal.

DRL Coachlines (888/263-1854, www.drl-lr.com), which makes the overland trip from St. John's to Port aux Basques daily, stops at Gander International Airport.

Gander lies on the TransCanada Highway, roughly 64 kilometers (and under an hour's drive) west of Terra Nova National Park and roughly 335 kilometers and a four-hour drive from St. John's.

GRAND FALLS-WINDSOR AND VICINITY

The next stopping point along the TransCanada Highway is Grand Falls-Windsor (www. townofgrandfallswindsor.com) and the clutch of towns nearby, which offer a mix of culture, history, and outdoor recreation.

Sights

The **Mary March Provincial Museum** (24 St. Catherine Road, Grand Falls-Windsor, 709/292-4522, www.therooms.ca, daily April 24–Oct.13, $2.50) is named after the very last Beothuk known to have been alive. The museum reveals the history and displays artifacts of Mary March's people, as well as of more recent events that took place in the region.

Sports and Recreation

Rafting Newfoundland (709/486-0892, www. raftingnewfoundland.com, $99 adults, $79 children, May–Oct.), at Aspen Brook 20 kilometers west of Grand Falls-Windsor, takes rafters down the fast chutes of Badger Brook every day for a six-hour trip, with picnic lunches provided on a rocky island halfway through the trip.

In Bishop's Falls, north of Grand Falls-Windsor, **Brookdale Adventures** (10 Main Street, Bishop's Falls, 709 258-7377, www. brookdaleinn.com) runs sightseeing and snowmobile tours up and down the near-pristine salmon habitat of the Exploits Valley.

Serious golfers can find links at the **Grand Falls Golf Club** (TransCanada Highway, 709/489-7631, www.grandfallsgolf.com,

May–Oct., $23 9 holes, $40 18 holes), located two kilometers west of Grand Falls-Windsor. Less serious golfers can go to an indoor 18-hole glow-in-the-dark course at **Glo to the Xtreme** (8 Station Road, Grand Falls-Windsor, www.glotothextreme.com, 11 A.M.–11 P.M. Mon.–Thurs., 11 A.M.–midnight Fri. and Sat., 2–10 P.M. Sun., $6.20 adults, $5.31 children).

Entertainment and Events

The **Queen Street Dinner Theatre** (8 Queen Street, Grand Falls-Windsor, 709/489-6560, www.andco.nf.ca) offers shows for eight weeks in the summer, as well as a Christmas special.

In mid-July, the **Exploits Valley Salmon Festival** (www.salmonfestival.com) is a five-day music festival to celebrate the Atlantic salmon migration, highlighting the importance of this fish to the region.

Accommodations

The **Highliner Country Inn** (Exit 17, TransCanada Highway, 709489-9611, $90–150) has 18 rooms available off the TCH west of Grand Falls-Windsor. This also serves as the Grand Falls-Windsor stop for the DRL Coachline bus.

The 22-room **Hotel Robin Hood** (78 Lincoln Road, Grand Falls-Windsor, 709/489-5324, www.hotelrobinhood.com, $100–120) offers standard amenities, plus a free continental breakfast.

Also by the TCH, the **Exploits Motel** (Bishop's Falls, 709/258-6665, www.exploits-motel.com, $80–130), with 24 rooms, adds a few touches, like a small fireplace, to its basic lodgings.

Getting There

Grand Falls-Windsor is roughly 100 kilometers west of Gander on the TransCanada Highway, an hour or so by car.

DRL Coachlines (888/263-1854, www.drl-lr.com), which makes the overland trip from St. John's to Port aux Basques daily, stops at Loder's Irving gas station in Bishop's Falls and the Highliner Country Inn in Grand Falls-Windsor.

Iceberg Alley and the Great Whale Coast

Two of the most popular sights in central Newfoundland for both visitors and residents alike are actually located in the sea off the north shore in areas known as Iceberg Alley and the Great Whale Coast.

The Atlantic Ocean to the north off central Newfoundland teems with whales of all species, including minke, humpback, and orca, as well as the smaller belugas and dolphins. As well, icebergs that break off glaciers in faraway Greenland fjords are carried hundreds of kilometers south by the cold Labrador Current to sweep past the coast of Newfoundland before melting in warmer southern waters—if they don't first get grounded on rocky shoals off the land jutting out from Newfoundland.

While plentiful tours are available to take you out on the water, these sights can be enjoyed even from the shore. Many of the towns lining the Atlantic from Musgrave Harbour in the east, to the islands northwest of Lewisporte, and to the Baie Verte Peninsula in the west have dozens of hiking trails and coastal prospects. You can find marked lookout trails in various spots such as Twillingate and in particular Fogo Island. With luck and the right season, you may have a spectacular view of whales breaching out of the water and of majestic mountains of ice drifting silently by or stuck on the ocean bottom, crumbling noisily under the summer sun. The so-called iceberg season is April–July, with May and June the best months to spot them.

Routes 320, 330, and 340 join into two large loops that provide about 300 kilometers of highway around the this, connecting towns like New-Wes-Valley and Musgrave Harbour to Twillingate and Change Islands.

TWILLINGATE

Often called the Iceberg Capital of the World, Twillingate have a prime spot on the coast facing the Atlantic. Made up of a north island and a south island, also called the Twillingate Islands, Twillingate makes it easy for you to pursue a quest to see icebergs and whales, with various lookouts, trails, and boat tours. However, there are also a few museums worth stopping to see, too.

Sights

The town of Twillingate is an old outport village that grew into a thriving fishing town, and its many bays and coves still host family-owned wharves and stages as they've done for hundreds of years. Here, the **Twillingate Museum** (Twillingate, 709/884-2825, www.tmacs.ca, daily May–Oct.) is a seasonally open treasure house of the region's long and fascinating history. Some exhibits are dedicated to local luminaries, and one shows artifacts from a Maritime Archaic Indian site excavated not far from the museum.

The **Long Point Lighthouse,** at the end of Route 340, offers views of the ocean from its viewing platform. From here, you may be able to spot whales, seabirds, and even an iceberg.

Those wishing to explore the story of the Beothuk, Newfoundland's extinct First Nation, can do so on their way in or out of Twillingate. Located in Boyd's Cove, where Route 340 heads out to the islands (40 kilometers north of the TransCanada Highway), the **Beothuk Interpretation Centre** (Route 340, Boyd's Cove, 709/656-3114, www.seethesites. ca, 10 A.M.–5:30 P.M. daily late May–early October, $3) tells and displays the tragic history of the vanished people, and a bronze statue depicting one of the last of the Beothuks can be reached on a short walking trail.

Hiking

There are a number of trails in Twillingate that explore nature and scenery. One example is the **Long Point Trail,** which gives the opportunity to see icebergs and an old copper mine. Starting at the parking lot of Long

WESTERN NEWFOUNDLAND

© MICHAEL JOHANSEN

Twillingate Museum

WESTERN NEWFOUNDLAND

© MICHAEL JOHANSEN

shops in Twillingate

Point Lighthouse going out to Sleepy Cove, this moderately difficult hike will take about three hours.

Boat Tours

For those not content to view from land, boat tours can bring people closer to the whales and icebergs. **Iceberg Quest Ocean Tours** (Pier 52, 52 Main Street, 709/884-1888, www.icebergquest.com, May–Sept., $44 adults, $22 children) sails with as many as 40 passengers four times a day from out into Notre Dame Bay to see icebergs, whales, and seabirds on a two-hour tour.

Twillingate Adventure Tours (128 Main Street, 709/884-5999, www.twillingateadventuretours.com, May–Sept.) sails the 55-foot, 40-passenger MV *Daybreak* four times a day, including a sunset cruise.

There's also **Twillingate Island Boat Tours** (50A Main Street, 800/611-2374, www.icebergtours.ca) that can take up to 20 people, three times a day on board the MV *Iceberg Alley* for a two-hour tour. Its hard-to-miss building also contains a craft shop offering locally made souvenirs.

Festivals

In late July, **Twillingate/New World Island Fish, Fun, and Folk Festival** (709/884-2174, www.fishfunfolkfestival.com) offers traditional Newfoundland music, a giant craft show, and fireworks.

Accommodations

Small bed-and-breakfasts make up the bulk of the offerings in Twillingate. For motel-type accommodations, the 22-room **Anchor Inn** (Twillingate, 709/884-2777, www.anchorinnmotel.ca, $92) offers rooms and suites.

Getting There

To get to Twillingate from Gander, take Route 330 north to Route 331 and change to Route 340 at Boyd's Cove. It's a 90-kilometer, 1.5-hour drive.

◖ FOGO ISLAND

The largest of its neighbors, Fogo Island (www.fogoisland.net) has history as well as great views for people making it to one of the ends of the Earth—which it is, according to the Flat Earth Society.

© MICHAEL JOHANSEN

This well-preserved outport house illustrates Newfoundland's traditional architectural style.

WESTERN NEWFOUNDLAND

There are 11 communities on Fogo Island, either on the main road or off on one of the exits. Stag Harbour is where the ferry docks, and Tilting is at the end of the road, farthest from the ferry. The town of Fogo has some notable hiking trails, and Joe Batt's Arm is the largest community on the island.

Hiking

Hiking trails crisscross many parts of the island, often affording spectacular views and possibly a whale or iceberg sighting. The 3.6-kilometer **Fogo Head Trail** starts in the town of Fogo and takes you up a great many stairs (400) to a view of the ocean. The **Groswater Trail** is a 1.6-kilometer walk Etheridge's Point Park in Joe Batt's Arm, where the sea stretches out before you. In Tilting, **Oliver's Cove** also has viewing potential and takes you to one of the island's abandoned towns.

Tours

The **Fogo Island and Change Island Adventure Boat Tours** (709/266-2392, www. fogotours.com, June–Sept., $15–40) runs passengers from the Ferry Dock in Stag Harbour, the Floating Wharf at Fogo Harbour and from the Government Wharf on the north side of Joe Batt's Arm to historic and beautiful Brimstone Head. Tours are offered four times a day.

As well, **Nicole's Picnics and Bicycle Tours** (159 Main Road, Joe Batt's Arm, 709/658-3663, www.nicolescafe.ca, June–Sept.) does as advertised (rents pedal bikes and provides picnic lunches).

Entertainment and Events

The **World's End Theatre Company** (709/743-4130, www.worldsendtheatre.org) puts on plays as well as the World's End Theatre Festival.

The **Brimstone Head Folk Festival** (Brimstone Head Park, Route 333, Fogo, www. town-fogo.ca) takes place in August and offers traditional musicians from Newfoundland and Ireland.

Accommodations

Fogo Island is not brimming with places to stay. The 11-room **Quiet Cannon Hotel** (Stag Harbour, 709/627-3477, $91) by Man O'War Cove is one option for basic accommodations.

Getting There

From Gander, take Route 330 to Route 331 and finally 335, which ends at the community of Farewell. From Farewell, the **Fogo Island Ferry** (709/535-6244 or 888/638-5454, www.tw.gov.nl.ca/ferryservices, $5.50 adults, $3.75 seniors and children 5–12, $16.50 car and driver) carries cars and passengers on the 45-minute ride to the island.

Coast of Bays

A trip to the southern Coast of Bays (www. coastofbays.nl.ca) brings travelers through the heart of Newfoundland to some of the most remote and scenic shoreline on the island.

CONNE RIVER AND VICINTY

Conne River is an ideal place to learn about the history of Canada's First Nations and to encounter a vibrant culture.

Miawpukek First Nation

The Miawpukek First Nation (Conne River, 709/882-2470, www.mfngov.ca) is the only native Canadian reserve on the island of Newfoundland and is home to several hundred Newfoundland Mi'kmaq. Both traditional and contemporary Mi'kmaq arts, crafts, writings, and music can be seen and experienced around the community. These are also offered for sale at various local outlets like the **Mi'kmaq Craft Shop** and the **Glenn John Arts and Craft Centre.**

Every year on the first weekend of July, the people of Conne River host a celebratory pow-wow that attracts drummers, dancers, singers, and spectators from all over North America.

Getting There

Take Route 360 due south from Bishop's Falls for almost 200 kilometers, then go west for 20 kilometers on Route 365 to get to Conne River.

Vicinity of Conne River

Visitors already in the area can drop in at the **Mikmaw Discovery Centre,** located where Route 360 meets Route 361 (the road to the town of St. Alban's). The Discovery Centre houses a giftshop, an art gallery, and the region's historical archives.

While there, visitors can get their tourism questions answered and be directed to the nearby **Jipujij'kuei Keuspem Nature Park** (709/538-8776), which features trails, beautiful beaches, and a re-creation of a traditional Mi'kmaq village.

Accommodations can be had in St. Albans, 42 kilometers from Conne River, at the 19-room **St. Alban's Inn.**

BAY DU NORD WILDERNESS RESERVE

With almost 3,000 square kilometers of territory, the Bay du Nord Wilderness Reserve (www.env.gov.nl.ca), along with the 600-square-kilometer Middle Ridge Wildlife Reserve that runs along its western border, is the largest protected area on the island, but it's also one of the most difficult to visit, located as it is in the roadless hills east of Route 360.

However, what makes the area a destination of choice is the Bay du Nord River that starts in both reserves and flows south to the shores of Belle Bay. The Bay du Nord was declared a Canadian Heritage River in 2005 to reflect its important cultural history and preserve its barely touched natural state.

Getting There

Visitors can only enter the protected reserves on foot or in a canoe. There are three hike-in access points; the park recommends taking the route from Piper's Hole River, coming from the east and following a transmission line.

Travel permits are free, but they must be obtained beforehand from **Notre Dame Provincial Park** (709/535-6632), or by contacting the provincial government's **Parks and Natural Areas Division** (709/635-4520).

Deer Lake to Port au Port Peninsula

As the TransCanada Highway enters western Newfoundland, it hits Deer Lake and moves south toward Port aux Basques, passing near Corner Brook and the Port au Port Peninsula accessed by a detour onto Route 460.

DEER LAKE

Deer Lake is a small gateway town to Gros Morne National Park, one of the biggest draws in western Newfoundland.

Sights

The **Newfoundland Insectarium and Butterfly Pavilion** (2 Bonne Bay Road, Reidville, 709/635-4545, www.nfinsectarium.com, mid-May–mid-Oct, 9 A.M.–6 P.M. daily summer, 9 A.M.–5 P.M. Mon.–Fri., 10 A.M.–5 P.M. Sat., noon–5 P.M. Sun. spring and fall, $10.50 adults, $9 seniors, $7 children) displays hundreds of mounted and live insect specimens. Reidville is less than half a kilometer north of Deer Lake on Route 430.

Sports and Recreation

Gros Morne National Park and all its recreational offerings is just a little more than 30 kilometers away from Deer Lake.

For golf, the **Humber River Golf Club** (21 Airport Road, Deer Lake, 709/635-5955, $40 18 holes) offers a relaxed atmosphere, catering to golfers of all ages and skill levels.

Festivals and Events

Deer Lake has the **Strawberry Festival Days** (www.town.deerlake.nf.ca) at the end of July for anyone who wants to taste some of the best strawberries in the world.

Accommodations

Deer Lake has several bed-and-breakfasts that offer reasonably priced accommodations. One such example is the three-room **Birchwood B&B** (14 Birch Street, 709/635-3116, $55).

In addition, Deer Lake has two main hotels. The 56-room **Deer Lake Motel** (15 TransCanada Highway, 800/563-2144, www.deerlakemotel.com, $89–139 rooms, $175 suites) offers standard rooms a short distance from the airport. The older, but comfortable and homier **Driftwood Inn** (3 Upper Nicholsville Road, 888/635-5115, www.driftwoodinn.ca, $89–96) has 24 rooms in a white and brown building.

Getting There

The **Deer Lake Airport** (www.deerlakeairport.com) is a regional airport located off the TransCanada Highway north of town. Air Canada, as well as three other regional and seasonal carriers, offers flights to Deer Lake.

DRL Coachlines (888/263-1854, www.drl-lr.com), which makes the overland trip from St. John's to Port aux Basques daily, stops at the Irving Big Stop station in Deer Lake.

Deer Lake lies along the TransCanada Highway and is located 270 kilometers from Port aux Basques, where the Marine Atlantic ferry from Nova Scotia docks. The drive between Port aux Basques and Deer Lake takes less than three hours.

CORNER BROOK AND VICINITY

Corner Brook is the largest town for many kilometers in western Newfoundland.

Sights

The **Railway Society of Newfoundland** (Station Road, 709/634-2720) is an old station converted into a train museum in Corner Brook that displays a steam engine, a working diesel-electric locomotive, and an unusual necessity in Canada: a snowplow train. Engine Number 593 once pulled the Newfie Bullet (as Newfoundland's notoriously slow train was affectionately called) from Port aux Basques to St. John's, but it's now on of the items on display at the museum.

The **Corner Brook Museum and Archives**

WESTERN NEWFOUNDLAND

CORNER BROOK

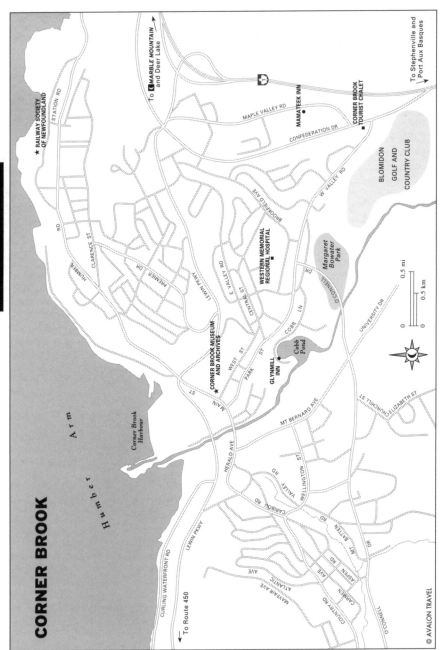

Humber Arm

Corner Brook Harbour

To Route 450

CURLING WATERFRONT RD

LEWIN PKWY

MAYFAIR AVE

ATLANTIC AVE

CARMEN AVE

ASPEN RD

COUNTRY RD

MT. BATTEN RD

DR

O'CONNELL

WELLINGTON ST

VALLEY RD

CARIBOU RD

HERALD AVE

MT BERNARD AVE

CHURCHILL ST

ELIZABETH ST

UNIVERSITY DR

★ RAILWAY SOCIETY OF NEWFOUNDLAND

STATION RD

HUMBER RD

CLARENCE ST

PREMIER DR

LEWIN PKWY

E VALLEY RD

CENTRAL ST

WEST ST

PARK ST

MAIN ST

★ CORNER BROOK MUSEUM AND ARCHIVES

GLYNMILL INN

Cobb Pond

COBB LN

O'CONNELL DR

■ WESTERN MEMORIAL REGIONAL HOSPITAL

BROOKFIELD AVE

Margaret Bowater Park

W VALLEY RD

CONFEDERATION DR

MAPLE VALLEY RD

MAMATEEK INN ●

■ CORNER BROOK TOURIST CHALET

BLOMIDON GOLF AND COUNTRY CLUB

To MARBLE MOUNTAIN and Deer Lake

To Stephenville and Port Aux Basques

0   0.5 mi
0   0.5 km

© AVALON TRAVEL

(2 West Street, 709/634-2518, www.cornerbrookmuseum.ca, $5 adults, $3 students, free children under 12) displays numerous artifacts connected with the long history of this large port town, its timber economy, and the people who've lived and worked here for centuries.

【 Grand Lake

Three reserves surround the southern half of the 60-kilometer-long Grand Lake (709/635-4520, www.env.gov.nl.ca), the largest body of fresh water on the island of Newfoundland. The waters are good for boating and fishing. The **Little Grand Lake Ecological Reserve,** the **Little Grand Lake Wildlife Reserve,** and the **Glover Island Public Reserve** protect hundreds of square kilometers of wilderness habitat, but are still open for limited public use. Services are few, but rewards to the traveler are many.

East of Corner Brook and Stephenville, Grand Lake is accessible by road along Route 480 and by boat south from the town of Howley on Route 401.

Golf

The **Blomidon Golf and Country Club** (West Valley Road, www.blomidongolf.com, 709/634-2523, May–Oct., $47 greens fee, $35 power cart rental) offers 18 holes right in the city of Corner Brook, with views as well.

North of town by the TransCanada Highway is the **Humber Valley Resort's River Course** (Exit 11, TransCanada Highway, 709/686-2710, www.humbervalley.com/golf.asp, $77 greens fee including power cart), a championship 18-hole, par-72 golf course that's 7,199 yards long in total.

Boat Tours

In the west end of Corner Brook at the Bay of Islands Yacht Club, **Crystal Waters Boat Tours** (Bay of Islands Yacht Club, 866/344-9808, www.crystalwatersboattours.com, 2–2.5 hours, $40–45 adults, $30 seniors, $25 students, $15–20 children 2–15) can sail with as many as 44 passengers to view the coves and inlets beneath the Blow-Me-Down Mountains and to spot whales and seabirds in the Gulf of St. Lawrence.

Festivals and Events

Cox's Cove, at the end of Route 440 north of Corner Brook, hosts the **Big Hill Festival** that showcases many talented local musicians at the end of July.

The other arts aren't left out, either. In mid-March, Corner Brook hosts the **March Hare** (themarchhare.ca), which is a festival of poetry, literature, film, and music that takes place at venues throughout the city.

More generally, Corner Book has a **Winter Carnival** (709/632-5343, http://cornerbrookwintercarnival.squarespace.com) in late February, which combines fireworks, snow sculptures, Newfoundland food, and variety shows with days of skiing at Marble Mountain.

Accommodations and Food

For an incredible view of Corner Brook and the Humber Arm (including the occasional iceberg), the **Mamateek Inn** (64 Maple Valley Road, 800/563-8600, www.mamateekinn.ca, $100–120) is not far off the TransCanada Highway and offers 55 rooms. The on-site My Brother's Place is a casual restaurant with breakfast available throughout the day.

Glynmill Inn (1B Cobb Lane, 800/563-4400, www.glynmillinn.ca, $103–190) rents out 78 rooms in a heritage building. For food, there's the Carriage Room, which serves traditional local cuisine at breakfast, lunch, and dinner.

The **Comfort Inn** (41 Maple Valley Drive, 800/228-5150, www.comfortinn.com, $115–160) has 78 rooms and standard accommodations.

During the summer months the **Sir Wilfred Grenfell College** (1 University Drive, 866/494-3548, www.swgc.mun.ca, $109–139), which is the Corner Brook campus of Memorial University, lets out its unused student residences, single rooms, and apartments to tourists.

Getting There

Corner Brook is located along the TransCanada Highway, with Exits 4–7 leading to the city. Deer Lake is 55 kilometers to the east, and Port aux Basques is 220 kilometers to the southwest.

DRL Coachlines (888/263-1854, www.drl-lr.com), which makes the overland trip from St. John's to Port aux Basques daily, stops at the Confederation Drive Irving station in Corner Brook.

◖ MARBLE MOUNTAIN

The premier winter sports and recreation destination in western Newfoundland, if not in all of Atlantic Canada, is the Marble Mountain Resort.

Skiing

The **Marble Mountain Resort** (709/637-7600, www.skimarble.com, day lift tickets $49 adults, $37 seniors and students, $25 children 5–12) offers first-class skiing. The mountain has five lifts and 37 runs on a 1,700-foot vertical drop and boasts enough snow (a 16-foot annual average) to please any number of skiers and snowboarders. The season normally runs December 26–April 12, or as long as the snow lasts.

Other Recreation

Attached to the Marble Mountain Resort, but open year-round, is **Marble Zip Tours** (709/632-5463, www.marbleziptours.com, $79 adults, $69 children). Those without fear of heights (and perhaps the braver of those with) are dressed in harnesses and slide down a series of six zip lines from platform to platform from the top of Marble Mountain down across **Steady Brook Gorge,** past beautiful waterfalls. The guided descent lasts about three hours and reaches heights of 250 feet over the forest floor. All necessary safety equipment and instruction is provided.

Accommodations

Marble Villa (709/637-7666, www.skimarble.com/thevilla.asp, $129–259) is the only accommodations option on the mountain itself. It offers apartment-style rooms and some come with a fireplace. Other accommodations can be found in nearby Corner Brook or Deer Lake.

Getting There

Marble Mountain is located about 10 kilometers north of Corner Brook on the TransCanada Highway; take Exit 8 at Steady Brook.

PORT AU PORT PENINSULA

Newfoundland's Frenchest region, the residents of this large picturesque peninsula have retained the language, culture, and arts of their Gallic ancestors, and they're more than willing to share their legendary hospitality.

Stephenville, though not technically on the peninsula, serves as a gateway. On the peninsula itself, there's Cape St. George and Mainland (La Grand Terre).

Sights

The Cercle des Mémoires (Route 463, Mainland/La Grand Terre, 709/642-5254, 11 A.M.–6 P.M. daily July–Aug.) is a museum in the Centre Scolaire et Communautaire in the village of St. Anne that explores Newfoundland's rich French history.

Sports and Recreation

Nine holes can be found at Black Duck Siding on Route 460 near Stephenville. **Dhoon Lodge Golfing** (Route 460, 709/646-5177, www.dhoonlodge.com) offers "stay and play" packages ($189 for one night) on a course surrounded by grassland and boreal forest.

Festivals and Events

To celebrate the shared culture of Newfoundland's English and French peoples, in early August there's the **Cape St. George and Mainland Regional Bilingual Folk Festival** (709/642-5254). In a similar vein, the **Black Duck Brook Festival** (709/642-5498) in mid-August also focuses on French and English arts. Black Duck Brook is located on route 463.

The first-class **Stephenville Theatre Festival** (129 Montana Drive, Stephenville,

709/643-4982, stf.nf.ca) features professional companies and lasts July–August with all performances held at the Stephenville Arts and Culture Centre.

Accommodations

Those stopping in Stephenville on their way to the Port au Port Peninsula have a number of choices for accommodations.

The **Holiday Inn** (Campbell Avenue, 44 Queen Street, Stephenville, 800/465-4329, www.holidayinnstephenville.com, $109–150) offers 47 basic rooms over two floors.

The 24-room **Hotel Stephenville** (19 Oregon Drive, Stephenville, 709/643-5176, www.hotelstephenville.com, $69–99) is located near many Stephenville attractions.

The five-room **Keyano Motel** (186 Hansen Memorial Hwy, Stephenville, 709/643-4600, $60–85) offers singles, doubles, and housekeeping units.

Getting There

Stephenville International Airport (13 Tennessee Drive, Stephenville, 709/643-8444, www.cyjt.com), on Route 490 close to the base of the Port au Port Peninsula, is a regional airport accommodating two airlines.

DRL Coachlines (888/263-1854, www.drl-lr.com), which makes the overland trip from St. John's to Port aux Basques daily, stops at the Crown Taxi stand in Stephenville.

Along Route 460 or Route 490, Stephenville is 165 kilometers north of Port aux Basques.

The Port au Port Peninsula lies west of Stephenville along Route 460 and Route 463.

Gros Morne National Park

Gros Morne National Park (709/458-2417, www.pc.gc.ca/grosmorne) is located west of Deer Lake in the heart of western Newfoundland, and it's often considered to be the centerpiece of the province's tourism industry. The park, a UNESCO World Heritage Site, protects some of the most beautiful of the island's natural wonders, including the Bonne Bay fjords and the Tableland mountains, along almost 100 kilometers of Newfoundland's west coast. It's a destination of choice for campers, hikers, cross-country skiers, and kayakers.

SIGHTS

Spread over 1,800 square kilometers, Gros Morne National Park stretches between the Gulf of St. Lawrence and the Long Range Mountains. Bonne Bay—with its East and South Arms—essentially splits the park into its north region, accessed via Route 430, and its south region, accessed via Route 431.

Several towns, most notably Rocky Harbour, Norris Point, and Woody Point, lie as enclaves in the park and are treated by Parks Canada as part of the Gros Morne experience.

Norris Point

Sitting on a point jutting out into Bonne Bay, the town of Norris Point (www.norrispoint.ca) is on the north side of the bay, six kilometers from the park visitors center off Route 430. It can best be seen from the 85-year-old **Jenniex House** (104 Main St., 709/458-2896), a location that provides a sweeping view over the town, the bay and the mountains. Jenniex House is also a good place to stop for some tea.

Another popular destination in Norris Point is the **Bonne Bay Marine Station** (1 Clarke's Lane, 709/458-2550, www.bonnebay.ca, May–Oct.), where visitors can view the life in a saltwater aquarium and get up close and personal with the animals of the sea at the research station's saltwater touch tank.

◖ Bonne Bay Fjords

Two fjords comprise Bonne Bay. The cliffs and mountains along the South Arm and East Arm contribute to Gros Morne's impressive scenery, and views can be had from a number of points, including along Route 430 going through the

© MICHAEL JOHANSEN

stop sign in Norris Point

Morne Park are in Western Brook Pond. Cliffs rise up along the water to make for a breathtaking gorge. Boat tours offer great views. There's also the Western Brook Pond Trail (six kilometers round-trip), located 32 kilometers north of the visitors center on Route 430.

Tablelands

This geologic treasure exposes a layer of the earth that once sat beneath an ocean. The brownish color of the cliffs and stones come from peridotite, which is usually found one layer below the earth's crust, in the mantle. Route 431 passes through the Tablelands, and you can also get a view from the water on a boat tour. **The Tablelands Trail** (four kilometers round-trip) puts you in the austere-seeming area. Pick up the trail from a parking lot four-kilometers west of the Woody Point Discovery Centre along Route 431.

Woody Point

Woody Point is known for its century-old heritage buildings and an annual summer writing festival. There's also the **Discovery Centre** (Route 431 near Woody Point, 9 A.M.–5 P.M. daily late May–early Oct.), where visitors can learn more about the park before setting out to explore. It is located 34 kilometers from the park entrance, along Route 431.

Lighthouse

The **Cow Head Lighthouse** (709/243-2681) can be seen in a small enclave within Gros Morne National Park on Route 430, 53 kilometers north of the visitors center.

Arches Provincial Park

Not within the boundaries of Gros Morne National Park, Arches Provincial Park (www.env.gov.nl.ca/parks, June–Sept.) lies on Route 430, about 20 kilometers north of Gros Morne. A view over the Arches, an incredible formation that the pounding sea has been carving out of living rock for millennia, is reached from a roadside parking lot by a short trail. Overnight camping is not allowed, but picnic sites are available.

Southeast Hills, from around Lomond off Route 431, and on the five-kilometer Lookout Trail starting at the Discovery Center in Woody Point. Boat tours leaving from Norris Point are also a great way to experience the bay.

Rocky Harbour

The largest of the three towns within the park, Rocky Harbour (www.rockyharbour.ca) is a good place to stop for services and possibly stay the night but does not offer not much in the way of sights. It is located 39 kilometers from the park entrance (four kilometers from the visitors center), along Route 430.

You can get a sense of the way of life in this part of the world, with fishermen cleaning nets at the docks in Rocky Harbour. Newfoundland is becoming a popular tourist destination, but it's still home to many men and women who depend on the sea for their livelihoods, just as their ancestors had done for hundreds of years.

Western Brook Pond

Some of the most spectacular scenery in Gros

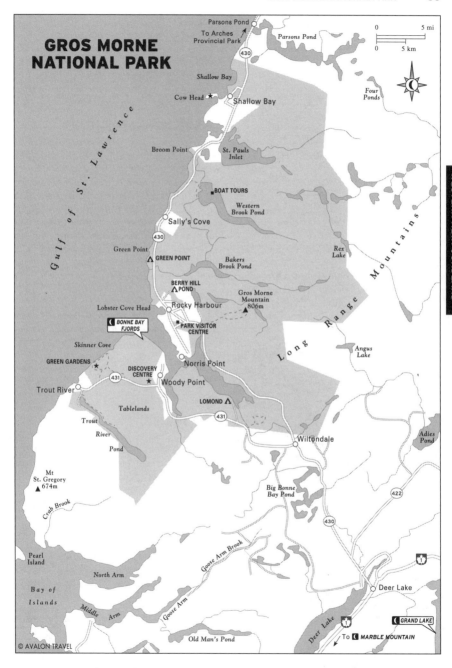

GROS MORNE NATIONAL PARK

Parsons Pond
To Arches
Provincial Park
Parsons Pond
430

0   5 mi
0   5 km

Shallow Bay

Cow Head   Shallow Bay

Four
Ponds

Broom Point   St. Pauls
Inlet

Gulf of St. Lawrence

BOAT TOURS

Western
Brook Pond

Sally's Cove

430

Rex
Lake

Green Point   GREEN POINT

Bakers
Brook Pond

BERRY HILL
POND

Gros Morne
Mountain
806m

Lobster Cove Head   Rocky Harbour

BONNE BAY
FJORDS

PARK VISITOR
CENTRE

Skinner Cove

GREEN GARDENS

Norris Point

Angus
Lake

DISCOVERY
CENTRE

Woody Point

Trout River

431

LOMOND

431

Tablelands

Long Range Mountains

Trout

River

Pond

Wiltondale

Adies
Pond

Mt
St. Gregory
674m

Big Bonne
Bay Pond

422

430

Crab Brook

Pearl
Island

North Arm

Deer Lake

Bay of
Islands

Goose Arm Brook

Goose Arm

Middle   Arm

GRAND LAKE

To MARBLE MOUNTAIN

Deer Lake

Old Man's Pond

© AVALON TRAVEL

SPORTS AND RECREATION
Hiking

Hiking trails have been built to give access to many of the park's natural features. The most popular, but strenuous, is the 16-kilometer climb up the 806-meter-tall **Gros Morne Mountain.** This hike can take 6–8 hours there and back, but a viewing platform equipped with restrooms is located at the half-way point. Start at the parking lot seven kilometers east of Rocky Harbour on Route 430.

Other trails include the two-kilometer **Old Mail Road** that explores the sand dunes by Shallow Bay. Start at the Shallow Bay picnic area, three kilometers north of Cow Head on Route 430.

The double-looped 25-kilometer **Green Gardens Trail** west of Woody Point takes hikers to the brink of high volcanic cliffs where they get impressive views over tall sea stacks. Start at either Wallace Brook Trailhead (11 kilometers west of Woody Point) or Long Pond

one of many hiking trails in Gros Morne National Park

Trailhead (13 kilometers west of Woody Point), both along Route 431.

The 10-kilometer trail around **Stuckless Pond** takes hikers into the Southeast Hills. Start at the trailhead 16 kilometers west of Wiltondale, off Route 431 going toward Woody Point.

Cross-Country Skiing

Groomed cross-country ski trails are located at five different sites throughout the park. The **Wigwam-Stuckless** trail, close to where Route 430 enters Gros Morne, provides the most skiing with almost 15 kilometers between and around three different ponds. Others are located at **Shallow Bay, Trout River, Berry Hill Pond,** and at the main **Visitor Centre** outside of Norris Point. The ski season usually lasts mid-January–early April. Winter camping is allowed at the Green Point Campground.

Golf

The **Gros Morne Resort Golf Course** (888/243-2644, www.grosmorneresort.com)—located in the northern half of the national park on Route 430 (between St. Paul's, which is 45 kilometers north of the visitors center, and Cow's Head)—has an 18-hole, par-72 course at the foot of the Long Range Mountains.

Boat Tours

Without doubt the most scenic boat tours in western Newfoundland are offered in the Gros Morne area, taking passengers up the ancient fjords of this spectacular coastline.

BonTours (888/458-2016, www.bontours.ca, daily June–Sept.) sails out of Norris Point and operates a number of tours and cruises in the park area for most of the year. The company runs the **Bonne Bay Tour** (two hours, $40 adults, $17 students, $14 children 11 and under) from Norris Point Dock to give views of the Tablelands and Gros Morne Mountain from the water. There's also a tour up the spectacular freshwater fjord of **Western Brook Pond** (two hours, $56 adults, $26 students, $21 children 11 and under), starting from the Western Brook Pond Dock, which

© MICHAEL JOHANSEN

requires a three-kilometer walk to reach. In July and August, BonTours offers the daytime **Bonne Bay Discovery Tour** (two hours, Mon., Wed., and Fri., $27 adults, $17 students) from Norris Point Dock for those wanting to learn about the marine ecosystem. The nighttime **Bonne Bay Evening Cruise** (Tues., Thurs., Sat., and Sun. July and Aug., $43) is for those who enjoy music, entertainment, and romantic sunsets.

Other Tours

Gros Morne Adventures (9 Clarke's Lane, Norris Point, 800/685-4624, www.grosmorneadventures.com) offers hiking, biking, kayaking, and winter tours starting at $50 per person.

Motorized winter tours can be arranged in the vicinity of Gros Morne National Park. **Funland Resort** (34 Veterans Dr., Cormak, 709/635-7227, www.funlandresort.com) offers packaged snowmobile tours through the Western Brook Gorge and up into the Lewis Hills. The tours take place December–April, snow permitting. Cormack is located on Route 422, which branches north off Route 430, a short distance from the TransCanada Highway between Deer Lake and Wiltondale.

Closer to the park, **Frontier Cottages** (Junction of Route 430 and Route 431, Wiltondale, 709/453-7266, www.frontiercottages.com) offers various guided snowmobile tours that are considered moderate to extreme in difficulty. Guides cost $250 per day for a party of no more than six snowmobilers.

Park Programs

Park staff organize activities throughout much of the year. Visitors can listen to music and stories performed at beachside campfires, follow interpreters and guides to learn about Gros Morne's cultural history and natural beauties, and meet local craftmakers and artists, including the official Artist in Residence—there's a new one every year. To get more information and schedules, inquire at the park visitors center or the Discovery Centre in Woody Point.

ENTERTAINMENT AND EVENTS
Festivals

Fans of world music can attend the "eclectic" **Gros Morne Summer Music Festival** (709/639-7293, www.gmsm.ca) at the Heritage Theatre (709/453-2304) in Woody Point and the Good Shepherd Anglican Church (709/458-2681) in Norris Point, held mid-July–mid-August every year.

Mid-August is the time for **Writers at Woody Point** (709/458-3388, http://writersatwoodypoint.com) in Gros Morne National Park. It takes place at the Woody Point Heritage Theatre (709/453-2304) and includes some music, but is mostly about books and writing.

The first-class **Gros Morne Theatre Festival** (709/639-7238, www.theatrenewfoundland.com/gmtf.html, June–Sept.) provides four months of drama, comedy, dinner theatre, recitations, and music at numerous venues in the town of Cow Head.

ACCOMMODATIONS AND FOOD

If Gros Morne National Park is your main destination in western Newfoundland, as it is for thousands of people a year, but you don't want to spend your whole stay sleeping under canvas (camping in a modern nylon tent, that is), many hotels and B&Bs can be found close at hand in most of the enclaved communities.

Norris Point

Norris Point has the 11-room **Sugar Hill Inn** (115-129 Sexton Road, 709/458-2147, www.sugarhillinn.nf.ca, $115–250), a hotel that offers luxurious accommodations and gourmet cooking in its dining room.

Jenniex House (104 Main St., 709/458-2896) is a good place to get locally picked berries, homemade muffins, and a good mug-up of tea.

Rocky Harbour

One of the best options is the 52-room **Ocean View Hotel** (38–42 Main Street, 709/458-2730 or 800/563-9887, www.theoceanview.ca, $125–165) on the waterfront in Rocky

Harbour—close to the main town docks where local inshore fishermen still land their catches. The hotel's **Ocean Dining Room** specializes in seafood and boasts a spectacular sunset view out past the Lobster Cove Head lighthouse—but it's also open for breakfast and lunch. The hotel's large **Anchor Lounge** is one of the most popular summer drinking establishments in the area, and it features an in-house band called Anchors Aweigh that plays traditional Newfoundland music two or three times a week. Ocean View Hotel closes at the end of October for the winter when business drops off, but it's often filled to capacity during the summer, so early reservations are recommended for the high season.

Rocky Harbour has several other places to stay. **Gros Morne Cabins** (Main Street, 709/458-2020, www.grosmornecabins.com, $119–189) has 25 one- or two-bedroom abodes with kitchens.

The six-room **Hilltop View B&B** (23 Ellsworth Lane, 709/458-2065, www.grosmorne.ca/hilltop, $65) is one of the less expensive places to sleep; each room has a queen bed.

There's also the four-room (plus one cottage) **Wildflowers Country Inn** (108 Main Street North, 709/458-3000, www.wildflowerscountryinn.ca, $89–159), a little bed-and-breakfast.

Woody Point

In Woody Point, **Seaside Suites** (39 Water Street, 709/638-5311, www.seasidesuites.ca, $159–219) offers three units on the waterfront—or "over the waterfront," as the hotel advertises, since the suites are built right over the water.

The **Lomond River Lodge** (Route 431 Lomond River, 877/456-6663, www.lomond-river-lodge.com, $55–125) rents out three rooms and six cabins, making for a more affordable option en-route to Woody Point.

Elsewhere in the Park

Elsewhere in Gros Morne Park, the **Gros Morne Resort** (888/243-2644, www.grosmorneresort.

com, $119–209), located Route 430 between St. Paul's, which is 45 kilometers north of the visitors center, and Cow's Head, offers guests use of a golf course with a stay in one of its rooms or suites.

The 82-unit **Shallow Bay Motel and Cabins** (Route 430, Cow Head, 800/563-1946, www.shallowbaymotel.com, $80–150) offers singles, doubles, and suites in Cow Head at the northern end of the national park.

Outside the Park

Just outside the south entrance to Gros Morne, are the **Frontier Cottages** (Junction of Route 430 and Route 431, Wiltondale, 709/453-7266, www.frontiercottages.com, $129–149), where at least one of the six cabins is equipped with a hot tub bath.

Campgrounds

Gros Morne Park has a total of five campgrounds (reservations 877/737-3783, www.pc-camping.ca, $18.60–25.50) accessible by car. Three campgrounds lie along Route 430 at **Berry Hill Pond** (69 sites, 10 kilometers from the visitors center), **Green Point** (31 sites, 17 kilometers north of the visitors center), and **Shallow Bay** (62 sites, 57 kilometers north of the visitors center. Two are accessible from Route 431 at **Lomond River** (25 drive-in and 4 walk-in sites, 17 kilometers west of the park entrance) and **Trout River Pond** (40 drive-in and 4 walk-in sites, 50 kilometers west of the park entrance). All have toilets and hot water except Green Point. Most are only open seasonally mid-June–mid-September, although Green Point is open year-round.

Backcountry campsites can be found on the **Snug Harbour, Lomond,** and **Green Gardens** trails. A backcountry permit and registration is necessary at the park visitors center.

INFORMATION AND SERVICES

The park entrance (late May–early October) is located in Wiltondale, 32 kilometers from Deer Lake along Route 430. Entrance fees are $9.80 adults, $8.30 seniors (over 65), $4.90 children

6–16, and $19.60 families (up to seven people in a vehicle). The park is open year-round, but many services and areas are closed in winter.

The park **visitors center** (709/458-2417, 9 A.M.–4 P.M. Mon.–Fri. early May–late May, 9 A.M.–5 P.M. daily late May–late June, early Sept.–late Oct., 9 A.M.–9 P.M. daily late June–early Sept., closed winter) is located 34 kilometers from Wiltondale along Route 430.

GETTING THERE AND AROUND

Gros Morne National Park lies along the Viking Trail (as Route 430 northwest of Deer Lake is known). The park entrance at Wiltondale is 32 kilometers northwest of Deer Lake along Route 430.

There are two main roads in the park. Route 430 takes you through the northern part of park and extends beyond the park all the way to St. Anthony on the Northern Peninsula. Norris Point, the park visitors center, Rocky Harbour, Shallow Bay, and Cow Head are accessed via Route 430.

Splitting off from Route 430 at Wiltondale, Route 431 runs through the southern part of the park. This road takes you to Woody Point and ends at Trout River.

By car, it takes about 1.5 hours to get from the Rocky Harbor/Norris Point area of the park to Woody Point. During July and August, you have the option of taking BonTour's seasonal shuttle boat from Norris Point across Bonne Bay to Woody Point.

Northern Peninsula

North from Gros Morne National Park, the Viking Trail, Route 430, continues up the Northern Peninsula to St. Anthony.

◖ PORT AU CHOIX

From western Newfoundland's natural history to its human history, the story begins at Port au Choix, where archaeologists have been uncovering artifacts and habitations from four ancient peoples, the oldest of which date back 5,500 years.

Sights

The **Port au Choix National Historic Site** (709/861-3522, http://parkscanada.gc.ca/portauchoix, 9 A.M.–6 P.M. daily June–Sept., $7.80 adults, $6.55 seniors, $3.90 children 6–16) displays archaeological exhibits in a visitors centre and offers guided tours and meetings with the archaeologists. A shoreline trail leads across limestone barrens and past old native burial grounds.

While in Port au Choix, you can also visit the **Heritage Centre** (Fisher Street, 709/861-3381, June–Sept. daily, free) on Fisher Street for an exploration of the more recent history of the town and the surrounding area. The museum

displays many antiques and artifacts once owned and used by members of local families.

Getting There

Port aux Choix lies west of Port Saunders on Route 430-28, about 230 kilometers north on the Viking Trail (110 kilometers north of Cows Head in Gros Morne National Park).

BIRD COVE
Sights

The **Bird Cove Interpretation Centre** (84–92 Michael's Drive, 709/247-2011, www.bigdroke.ca) is an interesting place that exhibits whale bones, fossils, and a display about the famous Captain James Cook who mapped much of Newfoundland's coastline.

Getting There

Bird Cove is located near the junction of 432, roughly 280 kilometers north of Deer Lake, on Route 430.

ST. BARBE

St. Barbe is the destination in the non-icy seasons of the MV *Apollo,* the passenger and car

WESTERN NEWFOUNDLAND

© MICHAEL JOHANSEN

The MV *Apollo* connects St. Barbe with the mainland territory of Labrador.

ferry that plies the Strait of Belle Isle, connecting the island of Newfoundland with mainland Canada. Visitors arriving or departing by ferry can find accommodations in St. Barbe.

Accommodations and Food

The most convenient accommodation is located within throwing distance of the Labrador Marine wharf. The 30-unit **Dockside Motel** (877/677-2444, www.docksidemotel.nf.ca, $75–120) offers 15 standard rooms, five executive suites (with hot tubs), and 10 fully equipped cottages. The hotel has a small lounge and a larger dining room that serves many Newfoundland dishes. Also, the main office of the Labrador Marine ferry terminal—where tickets are purchased and passengers can wait—is right on the premises.

Getting There

The MV *Apollo* passenger and car ferry crosses the Strait of Belle Isle, making the three-hour run between between Blanc Sablon, Quebec, and St. Barbe up to five times a day. The ferry,

run by **Labrador Marine Inc.** (866/535-2567 or 709/535-0810, www.labradormarine.com, $7.50 adults, $6 seniors and children, $22.75 vehicle and driver), operates all through summer and through most of spring and fall, depending on the ice conditions in the strait. Purchase tickets at the main office at the Dockside Motel.

St. Barbe is located 300 kilometers north of Deer Lake on Route 430.

L'ANSE AUX MEADOWS

Port au Choix and Gros Morne are important, but it's really L'Anse aux Meadows that puts western Newfoundland on the world map. The 1,000-year-old foundations of eight dwellings and workshops that were found here in the 1960s rewrote the history of two continents by proving that Norse Vikings sailed from Iceland and Greenland to settle on North American soil, albeit only for a short while.

Sights

Today, at the **L'Anse aux Meadows National**

© MICHAEL JOHANSEN

WESTERN NEWFOUNDLAND

a reconstructed Viking village at L'Anse aux Meadows

Historic Site (709/623-2608, http://park-scanada.gc.ca/meadows, 9 A.M.–6 P.M. daily June–Oct., $11.70 adults, $10.05 seniors, $5.80 children), the precious foundations of the Viking dwellings have been preserved under grassy mounds, and the artifacts found amongst them, like a soapstone spindle and a bronze pin, are on display with many other items in the newly renovated and up-dated Interpretation Centre. As well, several of the original Norse buildings—one of the dwelling halls and a couple of workshops, including the smithy—have been reconstructed nearby, and actors dressed as Vikings (sorry, no horned helmets) provide information and demonstrations of how the ill-fated settlers may have lived. L'Anse aux Meadows has been designated as a UNESCO World Heritage Site.

In the modern village of L'Anse aux Meadows, which is right beside the heritage site, another re-creation of a Norse settlement has been built at the **Norstead Viking Village** (709/623-2828, www.norstead.com, daily June–Sept., $10 adults, $8 seniors, $6 children). Norstead also features costumed actors who provide information and entertainment. It also has the *Snorri* on display—a re-created Viking ship that was actually sailed all the way from Greenland to Newfoundland to mark the 1,000-year anniversary of the L'Anse aux Meadows settlement. In June, the Norstead Viking Village holds the Summer Solstice Viking Festival with bonfires, storytellers, concerts, and games.

Outside L'Anse aux Meadows off Route 435, the **Cape Norman Lighthouse** is found as far north as you can get on the Northern Peninsula and is on one of the oldest lightstation sites in Canada, the first tower having been built there in 1865.

Getting There

L'Anse aux Meadows is located 42 kilometers from St. Anthony on Route 436.

ST. ANTHONY

Not far from L'Anse aux Meadows, the town of St. Anthony preserves the memory and much of the legacy of one of the most important men in the history of the Northern Peninsula and Labrador: the world-famous Sir Wilfred Grenfell. This English missionary established a medical base in St. Anthony more than a century ago and then set up nursing stations and hospitals in more than a dozen remote outports along two coasts. Grenfell's name is still on the provincial medical board that provides health care to the region.

Sights

The **Grenfell Interpretation Centre** (1 Maraval Road, 709/454-4010, www.grenfell-properties.com, 9 A.M.–5 P.M. Mon.–Fri., $10 adults, $8 seniors, $3 children) outlines Sir Wilfred's many contributions to the province and includes a gift shop.

Across the street from the Grenfell Interpretation Centre is the modern **Curtis Memorial Hospital** (178-200 West Street, 709/454-3333). The inside of the hospital's large round lobby is worth visiting as part of a Grenfell tour, since the curved walls are encircled by a beautiful and intricate clay mural depicting the man considers a medical hero and the many people he helped.

A short walk up the hill from the Curtis Memorial Hospital (parking is available at the Grenfell Interpretation Centre where all fees are paid), is the **Grenfell House** (709/454-4010, www.grenfell-properties.com, 9 A.M.–5 P.M. Mon.–Fri.), the home of Sir Wilfred and his wife. It is now converted into a museum dedicated to their lives and works.

Boat Tours

Northland Discovery Boat Tours (877/632-3747, www.discovernorthland.com, daily late May–early Oct., $55 adults, $10–28 children) sails into the northern waters of Iceberg Alley, where passengers can see bergs, caves, seabirds,

and many species of whales. Tours last about 2.5 hours and can accommodate up to 48 people.

Festivals and Events

St. Anthony hosts an **Iceberg Festival** (http://theicebergfestival.ca) in June to celebrate those beautiful floating white mountains by eating lots of traditional food and listening to lots of good music.

Accommodations and Food

St. Anthony's **Haven Inn** (14 Goose Cove Road, 877/428-3646, www.haveninn.ca, $92–133) offers 38 units (including two suites with hot tubs). Other services include a large-capacity lounge and special rate packages for snowmobilers. It also boasts a restaurant, **Cartier's Galley,** with the finest view in the area. The 40-seat restaurant overlooks much of the town and the busy harbour and serves traditional Newfoundland cuisine.

The **Grenfell Heritage Hotel** (1 McChada Drive, 888/450-8398, www.grenfellheritage-hotel.ca, $120) is a converted nursing residence located right beside the Grenfell Interpretation Centre. The hotel has 200 rooms and suites.

For something a little different and somewhat cheaper, the pretty **Fishing Point Bed and Breakfast** (Fishing Point Road, 866/454-2009, $80) has three rooms overlooking the entrance to the St. Anthony Harbour.

Getting There

St. Anthony is located at the end of the Viking Trail, which is more than 400 kilometers long, starting from Deer Lake, and the drive can take eight hours.

There is also the **St. Anthony Airport** (709/454-3192) on Route 430 near the junction of Route 432 for visitors wanting to arrive by plane.

Port aux Basques and the South Coast

Continuing south of Deer Lake and Corner Brook on the TransCanada Highway, drivers will eventually reach Port aux Basques. This may be the starting point for many as well, as Port aux Basques is the primary ferry entrance to western Newfoundland from mainland Canada.

PORT AUX BASQUES

Port aux Basques serves as the entry or exit point for visitors traveling by ferry. It is also lies at the western end of the TransCanada Highway on the island of Newfoundland.

Sights

West of Port aux Basques on Route 408 is the **Cape Ray Lightkeeper's House** (Lighthouse Road, Cape Ray, 709/695-7892 or 709/695-7411, 10 A.M.–8 P.M. daily late June–early Sept.) that serves as a museum of Dorset artifacts and is next door to the Cape Ray Lighthouse itself.

Festivals and Events

Port aux Basques has the **Feather and Folk Nature Festival** (http://featherandfolk.ca) in May, a popular event for birders from all over the region.

Accommodations

If entering western Newfoundland by ferry from the south, Port aux Basques has several hotels and B&Bs on offer.

The five rooms at **Heritage Home B&B** (11 Caribou Road, 709/695-3240, $65–75) are at the lower-priced end of the spectrum.

In addition to its 83 rooms, **St. Christopher's Hotel** (146 Caribou Road, 709/695-3500 or 800/563-4779, www.stchrishotel.com, $86–147) has a lounge and a fitness room.

The **Hotel Port aux Basques** (1 Grand Bay Road, 709/695-2171 or 877/695-2171, www.hotelpab.com, $85–119 rooms, $120–180 suites) overlooks Grand Bay and offers 49 rooms and suites.

Getting There

Many or even most travelers enter western Newfoundland at Port aux Basques on board a Marine Atlantic ferry sailing from North Sydney, Nova Scotia. **Marine Atlantic** (800/341-7981, www.marine-atlantic.ca, $34.35 adults, $31.37 seniors, $17.33 children 5–12) has a fleet of vessels it uses to make day (4.5–6 hours) and night (4.5–8 hours) crossings of Cabot Strait, weather permitting. All interprovincial ferries carry passengers and vehicles and offer cabins, game arcades, gift shops, restaurants, lounges that serve alcoholic beverages and feature live entertainment, and, of course, outdoor decks that offer wide views over a sparkling ocean, if the sun or the stars are shining.

Port aux Basques lies at the western end of the TransCanada Highway and is located 270 kilometers from Deer Lake. The drive between Port aux Basques and Deer Lake takes less than three hours.

DRL Coachlines (888/263-1854, www.drl-lr.com) starts and ends its daily overland trip to St. John's at the Marine Atlantic terminal in Port aux Basques.

SOUTH COAST

The 148-kilometer-long Route 480 runs from the TransCanada Highway east of Stephenville to Burgeo on the south coast.

Ramea

Anyone making the trip to Burgeo can then hop aboard a ferry to visit the beautiful island town of Ramea, but that will probably take more than a day.

The **Senior Puffins Museum** (5 Church Street, 709/625-2235) in Ramea was established with domestic artifacts and antiquarian books donated by a prominent local family and now tells the whole story of the remote island.

Rose Blanche

Rose Blanche is a town 45 kilometers east

THE APPALACHIAN TRAIL

Those who like to get around on foot can explore the newest sections of the International Appalachian Trail (www.iatnl.ca), which starts thousands of kilometers away in the southern U.S. state of Georgia. Newfoundland's Long Range Mountains form the northernmost ranges of the Appalachians, and they are the last to be included in the international trail system. When the work is done there will be about 1,200 kilometers to walk from Port aux Basques to L'Anse aux Meadows, but for now only four sections have been completed. Be among the first to walk through a vast untouched wilderness.

The first stretch starts at Port aux Basques along the TransCanada Trail. The second section, called the Indian Head Range Trail, is seven kilometers long and is suitable for moderate hiking. It starts off Route 460 between Stephenville Crossing and Noel's Pond and takes about half a day to walk, providing views over Bay St. George and the town of Stephenville. The third section, the Humber Valley Trail, runs 25 kilometers on hills beside the Humber River, with the trailhead off the TransCanada Highway between Corner Brook and the Humber Valley Resort. The last section to have been built so far, the Indian Lookout Trail, is a moderately difficult 35-kilometer hike up the Southwest Feeder Gulch. It starts just south of the Arches Provincial Park on Route 430.

of Port aux Basques, about a 30-minute drive on Route 470. The **Rose Blanche Lighthouse** (709/956-2052, www.roseblanchelighthouse.ca, 9 A.M.–9 P.M. daily summer, $3 adults, $2 children) is a restored granite lighthouse that was built in 1873 and recently restored.

From Rose Blanche, a passenger-only ferry travels along the south coast. Destinations include the communities of Little Bay, Grand Bruit, Burgeo, and eventually, after several transfers to other boats, the town of Hermitage on the Connaigre Peninsula. For reservations, rates, and sailing times, contact the **Marine Services Division** (709/891-1050, www.tw.gov.nl.ca/ferryservices).

LABRADOR

Labrador is the Big Land. Much of its 300,000 square kilometers remains unsettled wilderness, making it feel like one of the last frontiers of North America. Communities are separated by vast stretches of trees and water, some unreachable by land, relying on the skies and waters to get around. Where there are roads connecting towns, they are often unpaved, gravel tracks with hundreds of kilometers between services. Tourism boards often tout sitting on a beach at a manicured resort as "getting away from it all," but in Labrador, where town populations often number in the low hundreds (tiny L'Anse Amour has a population of seven), and cell phone reception is more the exception than the norm, you will truly be away.

This remoteness is one of the main draws of the region—and it will challenge your sense of adventure. Pristine rivers and rushing waterfalls, rugged mountains and uncut forests all await those with the time and the explorer's spirit to venture here.

But it's not as if there's not a human story here as well. The history of the people who once lived and now live here has a cast of characters that includes Innu, Inuit, Metis, Vikings, Basque whalers, and Moravians, as well as explorers, fisherfolk, and the militaries of the Allied powers of World War II. Their stories are told in museums and communities of Labrador.

PLANNING YOUR TIME

The Straits region in southern Labrador is the easiest to get to, with the Blanc Sablon and its ferry just over the Quebec border. This

© MICHAEL JOHANSEN

LABRADOR

HIGHLIGHTS

(**Point Amour Lighthouse:** Celebrated in story and song, the lighthouse on Point Amour (the Point of Love) was built of locally quarried limestone in 1858, and it still shines for sailors on the Strait of Belle Isle (page 68).

(**Pinware River Provincial Park:** The Pinware is a historic salmon river that rushes down one of the most spectacularly beautiful valleys in Labrador – and that says a lot (page 69).

(**Red Bay:** Only decades after Christopher Columbus first sailed to America, Basque whalers crossed the Atlantic Ocean in tiny wooden sailboats to hunt huge whales from a station in this sheltered bay on Labrador's Straits coast (page 69).

(**Battle Harbour:** At one time considered the capital of Labrador, this once-thriving commercial port fell on hard times and was eventually left abandoned. Fortunately, many of the original buildings survived and were restored to make the Battle Harbour National Historic District (page 71).

(**St. Lewis:** For those who like to go to extremes, this small town on the south coast of Labrador, northeast of Mary's Harbour, provides a unique opportunity: It's the farthest east anyone can drive on the continental mainland of North America (page 73).

(**Eagle River:** Famous worldwide for the size and health of the trout and Atlantic salmon that spawn in its headwaters, the Eagle River hosts several private and for-hire fishing lodges and is soon to be made into a provincial waterway park (page 76).

(**Muskrat Falls:** In a land that's full of rushing rivers and spectacular waterfalls, few can now rival the beauty and power of the massive rapids 30 kilometers west of Happy Valley-Goose Bay, where Muskrat Falls roar

around the sacred Innu site of Manitu-utshu (page 83).

(**Menihek Nordic Ski Club:** Labrador's premier cross-country ski club not only attracts top class skiers from all over the world but spawns them as well (page 86).

(**Torngat Mountains National Park:** Not for the faint of heart, the Torngat Mountains at the very northern tip of Labrador form Canada's newest national park and are the epitome of remoteness in an already remote region (page 91).

LOOK FOR (TO FIND RECOMMENDED SIGHTS AND ACTIVITIES.

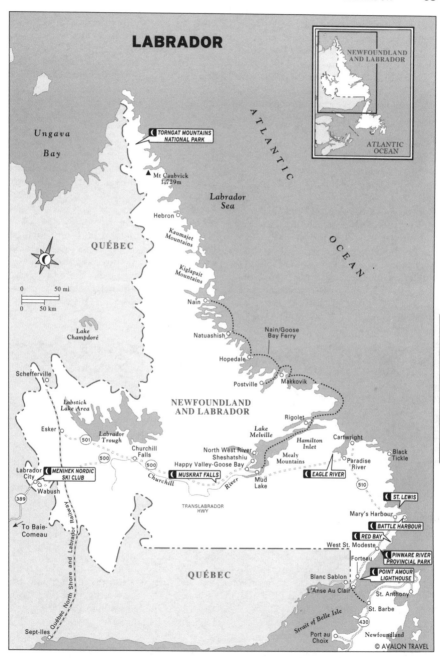

LABRADOR

NEWFOUNDLAND AND LABRADOR

ATLANTIC OCEAN

Ungava Bay

▲ Mt Caubvick 1,729m

TORNGAT MOUNTAINS NATIONAL PARK

Labrador Sea

Hebron

Kaumajet Mountains

QUÉBEC

Kiglapait Mountains

ATLANTIC OCEAN

Nain

Natuashish

Nain/Goose Bay Ferry

Hopedale

0   50 mi

0   50 km

Lake Champdoré

Postville   Makkovik

Schefferville

Labstick Lake Area

NEWFOUNDLAND AND LABRADOR

Rigolet

Lake Melville

Cartwright

Black Tickle

Esker   501

Labrador Trough

Churchill Falls   500   500

North West River Sheshatshiu

Happy Valley-Goose Bay

Hamilton Inlet

Mealy Mountains

Paradise River

510

Labrador City   MENIHEK NORDIC SKI CLUB

MUSKRAT FALLS

Churchill River

Mud Lake

EAGLE RIVER

ST. LEWIS

Wabush

389

Mary's Harbour

BATTLE HARBOUR

To Baie-Comeau

TRANSLABRADOR HWY

RED BAY

West St. Modeste

PINWARE RIVER PROVINCIAL PARK

Forteau

POINT AMOUR LIGHTHOUSE

QUÉBEC

Blanc Sablon

L'Anse Au Clair   St. Anthony

St. Barbe

Sept-Iles

Quebec North Shore and Labrador Railway

Strait of Belle Isle

Port au Choix   430   Newfoundland

© AVALON TRAVEL

LABRADOR

is also where the road, Route 510, is paved from L'Anse au Clair to Red Bay. In central Labrador, Happy Valley-Goose Bay, with its airport, is the hub community in the region.

North of Red Bay, the road turns to gravel and there's more of it between towns. This is true heading north to Cartwright and west from Port Hope Simpson to Happy Valley-Goose Bay. Even farther west, between Happy Valley-Goose Bay and Wabush, the roads are in the process of being paved, but still mostly gravel. All are encouraged to explore these newly opened highways, but anyone who does should know that their conditions aren't always good and they can become downright bad very quickly. Any kind of truck or passenger car can make the trip, but sturdier vehicles with high road clearance are generally preferred. Services for motorists are not readily available anywhere outside the Straits area or the other major communities, and cell phone signals don't reach many parts of Labrador. Always be prepared with extra spares, warm clothing, food, and possibly extra fuel.

Many regular drivers of the Labrador highway system carry satellite phones for emergency use. If you're broken down on the side of the road or otherwise in distress, don't hesitate to flag down the first person you see. Labradorians are famous for helping those in need.

Due to the remoteness, it's good to plan ahead. Some ferries, especially the one serving northern Labrador, can get filled with local travelers, so make reservations in advance. Traveling with outfitters or guides is advisable when exploring the wilderness areas like the Mealy Mountains, Eagle River, and Torngat Mountains in the far north. There are also seasonal considerations, since many places are not open outside the summer months.

It's best not to be in a hurry in Labrador. Unless you're flying (and those who do should know that prices are high, and the airline industry is in flux in Labrador), travel times are long, and driving the rough roads can get exhausting. When you're this far away, there's no need to rush.

The Straits

The paved portion of Route 510, also called the Labrador Coastal Trail, along the Straits is the oldest in Labrador and passes through some of the most densely populated coastline in the whole region. You'll pass more than a dozen communities with hundreds, even thousands of years of history behind them. The paved highway lasts as far as Red Bay, the easternmost of the clutch of towns hugging the Straight of Belle Isle that makes up the Straits region, a distance of 76 kilometers.

L'ANSE AU CLAIR

L'Anse au Clair is the first Labrador town across the border from Quebec, and Blanc Sablon is the town connected to the island of Newfoundland by ferry.

Sights

The first museum you'll find coming off the ferry in Blanc Sablon and driving east is the appropriately named **Gateway to Labrador Visitor Centre** (709/931-2013 or 877/931-2013, lshdc@labradorstraits.net, 9:30 A.M.–5:30 P.M. daily June–Sept. hours vary, free). The Centre is a restored wooden church dating from the early 1900s that you'll see on your right when you get to the bottom of the big hill coming into town. The Visitor Centre provides practical information for tourists, but also displays local artwork and artifacts that tell the story of 9,000 years of Labrador history.

Every Monday and Friday at 7:30 P.M. in July and August, when the summer sun still lasts long into the evening, visitors can join a two-hour **guided walking tour** (Northern Light Inn, 58 Main Street, 709/931-2332, $5) of L'Anse au Clair to learn about the lifestyles and traditions found in Labrador. The walk finishes up with tea and buns at Aunt Jessie's Kitchen.

Accommodations and Food

The first official place you'll find coming across the border from Quebec is the large and comfortable **Northern Light Inn** (58 Main Street, 709/931-2332 or 800/563-3188, www.northernlightinn.com, $89–169 rooms, $95–169 cottages). This 54-room hotel provides guests with a fine view over the town and the bay and is within walking distance of various stores and services, including the Gateway to Labrador Visitor Centre. The hotel also has five cottages it rents out all year-round, and it runs its own RV park. There's also a restaurant on site serving Labrador favorites.

L'Anse au Clair also has the three-room **Beachside Hospitality Home** (9 Lodge Road, 709/931-2338, $48–60, additional charges for extra guests), and traditional meals are prepared on request. The Hospitality Home is open year-round.

Getting There

From the Blanc Sablon Quebec ferry terminal, it's only a short drive east across the border to Labrador—or, indeed, a short walk if one takes the original road, the ancient Jersey Room Trail, that follows the rocky shoreline into L'Anse au Clair.

The MV *Apollo* passenger and car ferry crosses the Strait of Belle Isle, making the three-hour run between Blanc Sablon, Quebec, and St. Barbe, Newfoundland, up to five times a day. The ferry, run by **Labrador Marine Inc.** (866/535-2567 or 709/535-0810, www.labradormarine.com, $7.50 adults, $6 seniors and children, $22.75 vehicle and driver), operates all through summer and through most of spring and fall, depending on the ice conditions in the strait. In the winter months, Labrador Marine has recently begun using the MV *Sir Robert Bond* to carry freight, passengers, and vehicles between Corner Brook, Newfoundland, and Blanc Sablon two or three times a week.

FORTEAU

Forteau is northeast of L'Anse au Clair along Route 510 and offers activities related to the region's famous berries.

Recreation

Labrador Adventures (709/931-2055, www.tourlabrador.ca, mid-August–mid-September, $50 adults, $35 children) in Forteau heads to the hills every weekend to guide groups of visitors to pick wild Labrador berries—blueberries, redberries, bakeapples (the region's favourite berry)—and enjoy a large Labrador day with a hearty outdoor boil-up. Guests then return to town to make their own jam out of the berries they picked.

You'll forego the picking part, but **Seaview Restaurant** (Main Road, 709/931-2840, www.tourlabrador.ca) teaches how to take local berries, preserve them, prepare them, and cook with them. Group demonstrations must be scheduled beforehand by appointment.

Festival

A three-day festival in the first week of August, Forteau's **Bakeapple Folk Festival** (709/931-2097) uses the region's favourite berry as an excuse to feast and listen to live local music.

Accommodations and Food

There's a splendid place to stay in Forteau at the **Grenfell Louie A. Hall Bed and Breakfast** (709/931-2916, www.grenfellbandb.ca, $50–70, $10 per additional adult), which was a beautiful nursing station built in 1946 and lightly converted in 1994 to be used as tourist accommodations.

Forteau also has **Seaview Cabins and Suites** (Main Road, 866/931-2840, www.tourlabrador.ca, $89–100), open all year with eight oceanside units and an on-site restaurant.

Services

There is a detachment of the **Royal Canadian Mounted Police** (709/931-2790) in Forteau. There is also a branch of the **Labrador-Grenfell Health Corporation** (709/931-2450).

LABRADOR

Getting There

Forteau is 10 kilometers northeast of L'Anse au Clair on Route 510.

POINT AMOUR AND L'ANSE AMOUR

Point Amour is more than just the location of one of the oldest, most important and most beautiful lighthouses in Atlantic Canada (if not the whole country). It's also the site of the oldest known monumental graves in North America and it's home to one of the smallest, but most vibrant, villages anywhere.

◖ Point Amour Lighthouse

The Point Amour Lighthouse (L'Anse Amour Road, 709/927-5825, www.pointamourlighthouse.ca, 10 A.M.–5:30 P.M. daily late spring–early fall, $3 adults, free children 12 and under), now a Provincial Historic Site, took four years to build using limestone dug from local quarries. It was first lit in 1858, making it one of the oldest still-functioning lightstations in the world. At 109 feet tall, the Point Amour Lighthouse is the second highest in Canada, and a climb to the top of it provides an amazing view over the south coast of Labrador, the Strait of Belle Isle, and the northern tip of Newfoundland.

Other Sights

Past the lighthouse, farther down L'Anse Amour Road towards Fox Cove, is the **Maritime Archaic Burial Mound National Historic Site** (L'Anse Amour Road, 709/920-2142, year-round). Here, a 7,500-year-old burial mound was discovered to contain the skeleton of a child belonging to the ancient Maritime Archaic Indian culture. Since no older ceremonial graves like this one have been found anywhere else on the continent, that might make Labrador the cradle of aboriginal civilization.

Also on Point Amour, the **Heritage Research Centre** (L'Anse Amour Road, 709/931-2013 or 877/931-2013, www.pointamourlighthouse.ca) takes advantage of the immediate area's 8,000-year-old history to organize educational seminars, workshops, music camps, traditional craft demonstrations, live history theatre, and Sunday afternoon teas during all of July and August. Also, artists, students, and study groups can stay in hostel-style accommodations for a fee.

To get to the historical Point Amour sites off Route 510, you have to drive through the village of **L'Anse Amour** and the first thing you'll notice about it—besides how pretty it is beside the bay—is its particularly small size. As of the last national census, L'Anse Amour had an official population of only seven people—most of descended from the same family that first settled the point a long time ago.

A good place to rest and view the town of L'Anse Amour on a nice day is at a small picnic and barbecue site set up beside the community's welcome sign across the road from the village cemetery.

In L'Anse Amour, the **Labrador Straits Museum** (790/927-5873, www.labrador-straitsmuseum.ca, June 15–Sept. 15) not only displays historical artifacts and antiques used by local settlers to travel, hunt, fish, and just plain live, but it also sells a wide range of locally made handicrafts, including wool hats, leather moccasins, and hand-stitched quilts. Among the exhibited artifacts are an assortment of iron traps and the town of Forteau's very first feather bed.

Accommodations

Tiny L'Anse Amour has one place to stay: the three-room **Lighthouse Cove Bed and Breakfast** (L'Anse Amour, 709/927-5690, http://lighthousecovebb.labradorstraits.net, $40 single, $50 double). Guests must share a bathroom.

People wanting to stay in this vicinity might want to try L'Anse au Loup, the next town up Route 510, where travelers have a choice between two bed-and-breakfasts.

Barney's (122 Main Street, 709/927-5634, $45–50) has three rooms: Two rooms have one double bed each, and one larger room has both a double bed and a single bed. Home-cooked meals made from locally caught seafood are accompanied by homemade bread.

Marina's Harbour View B&B (10 Hillside Drive, 709/927-5881, $60) has four rooms with double beds and is open year-round. Marina's also serves homemade bread and fresh muffins with a full breakfast.

Getting There

Point Amour is easily found off Route 510 between Forteau and L'Anse au Loup. L'Anse Amour Road leads the way to the main sights.

WEST ST. MODESTE
【 Pinware River Provincial Park

The oldest protected area in Labrador is the Pinware River Provincial Park (709/927-5316, www.env.gov.nl.ca/parks, May–Sept.), which was opened in 1974 to protect 68 hectares of habitat and terrain in the Pinware River Valley northeast of West St. Modeste. The Pinware is a premier salmon river set in an amazingly beautiful gorge. The park provides 25 picnic sites, 15 tent sites with picnic tables, several convenient pit privies and drinking water taps, a comfort station, and a dumping station for RVs. The Pinware River Provincial Park is open most of the year for campers, and the river has several fishing lodges built along its upper reaches. The park is located off Route 510, roughly 35 kilometers southwest of Red Bay.

Labrador Culture Craft Shop

In West St. Modeste during July and August, the Labrador Culture Craft Shop hosts a two-hour program (709/927-5551, 7 A.M.–9 P.M. Tues. and Thurs., July and Aug.) that introduces visitors to Labrador's unique traditions and teaches them how to hook rugs and make molasses candy.

Accommodations

Located right on Route 510, the **Oceanview Resort** (Route 510, West St. Modeste, 709/927-5288, www.oceanviewresort.ca, $155 rooms, $105–145 cabins) offers 10 rooms and 4 log cabins, as well as a licensed lounge, a dining room, and gift shop, right on Route 510.

Getting There

West St. Modeste lies along Route 510, roughly 40 kilometers from L'Anse au Clair.

【 RED BAY

No less historically important or stunningly beautiful than any other in the Straits, the modern town of Red Bay—the easternmost community in the Straits area—has been settled for less than 200 years, but it was built on grounds first used by Basque whalers as early as the 16th century. At one time 500–1,000 men crossed the stormy North Atlantic every spring in tiny wooden boats in search of wealth. They summered at Red Bay, using the harbour as a base, the sheltered shoreline as an oil-processing station, and Saddle Island as their lookout for the great whales they hunted in the Strait of Belle Isle. In the fall they returned east in their heavily laden boats to sell the precious whale oil in Europe for hefty profits.

By the early 1600s most of the right and bowhead whales were gone from the Strait and

firewood tipis on a hillside above the town of Red Bay

© MICHAEL JOHANSEN

LABRADOR

LABRADOR

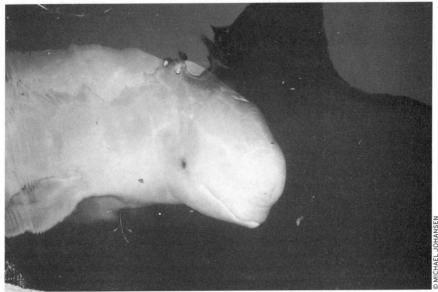

young beluga whale in the Red Bay harbour

the Basques stopped coming to Labrador. Gone and eventually forgotten, the whalers nonetheless left behind a wealth of artifacts sunken beneath the harbour waters and hidden underneath the surface of the land. Saddle Island held the graves of 140 men, and all the stony beaches around the bay are littered with ancient whalebones and thousands of once-mysterious pieces of hardened red clay—broken bits of the tiles the whalers had brought with them from Europe more than 400 years ago to roof their North American buildings.

Sights

Today the **Red Bay Historic Site** (Red Bay, 709/920-2142, www.pc.gc.ca/redbay, 9 a.m.–6 p.m. daily June–Sept., $7.80 adults, $6.55 seniors, $3.90 children) preserves and displays most of the artifacts recovered during an extensive series of archaeological digs on the land and underwater since the vanished Basque presence was discovered in the 1970s. Most notable is a relatively small boat called a chalupa, which was recovered—broken but

otherwise mostly intact—from underneath one of the four 16th-century galleons that have been discovered on the floor of the bay. The galleons themselves were left in place for their own protection.

The rebuilt chalupa, along with the giant skeletal fin of a right whale, is on display in the **Visitor Orientation Centre** at the top of the hill beside Red Bay's community church. The Orientation Centre is where to start the tour of the various historical sites. When you're done with the chalupa, you're sent a short distance down the hill to a second museum where most of Red Bay's recovered artifacts are on display alongside numerous models and re-creations.

Seeing, reading, and experiencing everything there takes about an hour, which is good because that'll make you just about ready to catch the next boat to **Saddle Island**—a vital and beautiful part of the Basque station that not only shows signs of the hundreds of years of European use, but also thousands of years of aboriginal presence. Parks Canada provides a map detailing all the major sites and digs on the island and the trails that lead to them all. The ferry boat makes a return trip from the Parks Canada docks at the lower museum to Saddle Island every hour every day during the tourist season, June–September.

Close to the Red Bay Interpretation Centre, but set up and operated by the local town council (not Parks Canada), is the **Red Bay Right Whale Exhibit** (Selma Baricham Town Centre, 50 Main Highway, 709/920-2197 Red Bay Town Office), which features the 400-year-old skeleton of a 60-foot right whale that had been discovered beneath the harbour floor, reassembled, and put on display in a protective environment.

Boat Tours

Just coming to Labrador is often an adventure in itself, but anyone who needs more can go with **Gull Island Charters** (18 East Harbour Drive, 709/920-2058, daily June–Sept.) and take to the seas where the Basques hunted whales more than 400 years ago. Gull Island offers tours and charters, taking passengers to see whales, seals, seabirds, icebergs, and other natural wonders along the northern shore of the Strait of Belle Isle.

Accommodations and Food

Red Bay has perhaps the most unique tourist accommodations in all of Labrador. **Whalers Restaurant, Gift Shop and Cabins** (709/920-2156, lstentltd@canada.com, $120) has taken several of the community's historic commercial buildings, restored them and refurbished them for use as hotel rooms. The cabins are not open year-round, but throughout summer and most of spring and autumn guests have a choice between the Loft, the Stagehead, the Strand House, and the Whaling Station Cabin.

Getting There

Red Bay is roughly 76 kilometers northeast of L'Anse au Clair, at the end of the paved portion of Route 510.

Southern Labrador

After Red Bay the towns of southern Labrador get more spread apart, and the roads turn into gravel. Anyone venturing on a drive north of Red Bay should not go unprepared—especially in the wintertime. It's always advisable to prepare for punctures, breakdowns, and strandings with extra spares, warm clothing, food, and possibly extra fuel.

From Red Bay to Cartwright, Route 510 is 338 kilometers of rough dirt road that can be driven in one hard day, but shouldn't be because there are too many interesting places to stop along the way—plus, that much driving on such a road is nothing less than exhausting. Gas stations are open in almost every community within sight of the highway, but drivers should definitely check how much fuel they have in their tanks if they're going north out of Port Hope Simpson. The next station is 200 kilometers away in Cartwright, and there's very little in between except for trees, water, and sky.

◖ BATTLE HARBOUR

For hundreds of years the primary destination for travelers and residents in southern Labrador was always the commercial centre at Battle Harbour. Everybody passed through the island town on their way by sailboat up and down the coast. The town grew rich and populous. Some people started calling it the capital of Labrador. However, as the years passed, the island lost its importance, and the prosperity faded away. Residents moved from Battle Harbour, many of them to nearby Mary's Harbour, in search of better livelihoods. Soon the whole community was abandoned and almost forgotten. Fortunately, Battle Harbour has once again become the place to go in Labrador, ever since the Battle Harbour Historic Trust was set up

LABRADOR

in the 1990s and began preserving all the old buildings that had survived.

Sights

Today the island is the **Battle Harbour National Historic District** (Battle Island, 709/921-6325, www.battleharbour.com, mid-June–mid-September, $9 adults, $7.65 seniors, $4.50 children 6–16) with many authentically and lovingly restored structures, including six heritage homes, several waterfront sheds and warehouses, and one general store. Guided walking tours (1.5–2 hours, once daily) are available, and visitors can also walk and look on their own. Guests are free to follow the island's many old footpaths or cross the narrow channel to explore other nearby abandoned settlements.

Festivals

Battle Harbour Fun Day (www.battleharbour.com) takes place on July 24 in the historic and restored island community. Fun Day is a garden party that celebrates Labrador heritage with traditional games and other entertainments.

Accommodations

Visitors can spend the day on the island or remain one or more nights in the one of the various accommodations (reservations@battleharbour.com). The **Battle Harbour Inn** ($150) has five rooms with shared bathrooms. There are four **cottages,** two of which can only be reserved as a whole ($190–245). The other two can be reserved as rooms ($135) with shared bathrooms or as a whole ($375–415). The **Cookhouse-Bunkhouse** ($35 single) has hostel-style berths.

Getting There

The facilities at Battle Harbour are open and staffed during the tourist season (mid-June–mid-Sept.) and at that time the island can be reached by a small scheduled ferry from the **Visitor Information Centre and Ferry Terminal** (Grenfell Mission wharf, Main Street, Mary's Harbour, 709/921-6325, www.battleharbour.com, $60 adults, $55 seniors, $30 children 6–16) in Mary's Harbour. The trip takes one hour, and the boat leaves at 11 A.M. and 6 P.M. daily. (The return trip leaves the island at 4 P.M. and 9 A.M. daily.)

wharf in Mary's Harbour

© MICHAEL JOHANSEN

LABRADOR

The island's marina provides a docking area for private pleasure craft.

Even though none of the buildings are open and there's nowhere to stay, people are still permitted to visit Battle Harbour in the off-season. Transportation can be arranged with private boat owners in Mary's Harbour for an average cost of around $50 a trip.

MARY'S HARBOUR

The first place to stop when driving north from Red Bay is Mary's Harbour. The town has services and is the departure point for visiting Battle Harbour.

Festivals

Crab is this community's fishing mainstay, and the **Mary's Harbour Crab Festival** (709/921-6929) celebrates the crustacean with a three-day weekend of fun during the first week of August.

Accommodations

The first place to stay driving north into southern Labrador is the **Riverlodge Hotel** (Main Road, 709/921-6948, $120). The Riverlodge has 15 rooms, a restaurant, and Old Pete's Lounge.

Mary's Harbour also has **Noel's Lodgings** (709/921-6444), which rents a number of housekeeping units and offers laundry facilities throughout the year.

Services

There is a detachment of the **Royal Canadian Mounted Police** (709/921-6229) in Mary's Harbour. There is also a branch of the **Labrador-Grenfell Health Corporation** (709/921-6228). The local **Eagle River Credit Union** (10–12 Hillview Road, 709/921-6354) has a branch in Mary's Harbour as well.

Getting There

Mary's Harbour is located roughly 65 kilometers north of Red Bay.

❰ ST. LEWIS

This small community is the farthest east you can get on a road on the North American mainland.

LABRADOR

© MICHAEL JOHANSEN

waterfalls near Mary's Harbour

Sights

Loder's Point Premises Museum (St. Lewis, 709/939-2266, 9 A.M.–8 P.M. daily mid-June–Aug., by appointment rest of year, free) can be found in St. Lewis. St. Lewis's museum has been set up inside the restored waterfront buildings and houses once used by a large mercantile business. The artifacts displayed are primarily connected with the region's centuries-old fishing industry, but other aspects of local history are also represented.

While in St. Lewis, you might want to follow the boardwalk that starts at the very end of Route 513 and leads to the Fisherman's Point Gazebo, a modern shelter that overlooks St. Lewis Sound, where often whales swim and icebergs float.

Getting There

St. Lewis is located at the end of 30-kilometer Route 513 that turns off Route 510 about 32 kilometers north of Mary's Harbour.

PORT HOPE SIMPSON

Port Hope Simpson is the last town before the long wilderness drive to either Cartwright or Happy Valley-Goose Bay. It offers places to stay as well as some services.

Festivals

In the middle of August or a little later, the island community of Williams Harbour celebrates a species of fish that only swims in their waters by holding the **Golden Cod Festival** (709/924-0287, www.gilbertbay.com) with two days of food and entertainment. Visitors can reach Williams Harbour by taking the Labrador Marine ferry from Port Hope Simpson.

Accommodations and Food

The 28-unit **Alexis Hotel** (709/960-0228, hotelalexis@gmail.com, $130 rooms, $185 suites) is the largest in town and has a licensed lounge and a restaurant on the premises. The hotel also organizes snowmobile tours (Jan.–Apr.) in the wilderness of southern Labrador and offers help to plan all other kinds of tours during the rest of the year.

Visitors to Port Hope Simpson can also stay at the four-room **Campbell's Place B&B** (98 Pioneer Street, 709/960-0606, $55–75), **PHS Lodgings** (709/960-0444), or **Russell's RV Park** (709/960-0405).

Services

There is a station of the **Labrador-Grenfell Health Corporation** (709/960-0271) in Port Hope Simpson.

Getting There

Port Hope Simpson is a little over 50 kilometers north of Mary's Harbour. Be sure to check your gas tank before leaving Port Hope Simpson, as Cartwright, your next chance to fill up, is 200 kilometers away.

CARTWRIGHT

It's no wonder where Cartwright gets its name: Captain George Cartwright founded the town in the late 1700s.

Sights

The Fequet General Store was one of Cartwright's original trading posts (it was established to compete against the Hudson's Bay Company), and the building—a large, two-storey wooden building on the old Cartwright waterfront where slim wharves once extended far out into the harbour and a few decaying warehouses still stand—is still owned by the family that founded it. The store is closed, but it has been converted into the private **Fequet's Museum** (Cartwright Town Council, 709/938-7259, free), displaying many of the region's historic and prehistoric artifacts. Everything to do with Cartwright's and Labrador's centuries-long history can be seen in Fequet's Museum, including tools, paddles, old musical instruments and radios, antique outboard motors, and election posters from the region's stormy political past. Viewing is possible by appointment only, and unfortunately such appointments are not always easy to get. A member of the family is usually happy to show visitors around the displays. As of this writing, the management of the Fequet's Museum was in the process of change.

© MICHAEL JOHANSEN

Fequet's Museum in Cartwright displays many of the region's historic and prehistoric artifacts.

LABRADOR

High above Cartwright on **Flagstaff Hill** are the two cannon that were first placed there in 1775 by Captain George Cartwright, who wanted to protect his settlers against attacks by privateers. The hill can be reached by a marked footpath that starts at the top of Flagstaff Lane; at the top of the hill, there's a large gazebo and a flagstaff that stands on the very spot of the original one it was named after.

For an even wider and higher view of the area south of Cartwright, visitors with sturdy boots or four-wheel-drive vehicles can go several kilometers up the barely maintained **Old Radar Base Road** to the top of a hill where the United States Air Force ran a radar station as part of the defensive continent-wide Pinetree Line during the years 1951 to 1968. Only the massive concrete foundations of the military structures remain, but one of the largest has been plaqued and converted into a tourist shelter, complete with picnic tables.

Back in town anyone wishing to pursue the Captain George Cartwright story should head to the old graveyard on the east side of town between Point Road and Willow Lane. The **cemetery** holds many of the town's early settlers and residents, but it also features the massive marble **George Cartwright Monument,** set in place (with the help of some workmen, one hopes) by the Captain's niece, Frances Dorothy Cartwright, more than a century ago.

Recreation

The remote **Gannet Islands Ecological Reserve** (709/635-4520, www.gov.nl.ca/parks) is a prime destination for serious birders and ornithologists, being as it is the protected seasonal home of more than 200,000 seabirds of many different kinds, including the largest colony of razorbills in North America. The Gannet Islands are more than 20 kilometers offshore, but can be approached by boat from Cartwright.

Boat Tours

Experience Labrador (20 Lethbridge Lane, 877/938-7444, www.experiencelabrador.com, daily June–Sept.), which is located on the bay shoreline on Lethbridge Lane off Main Road where it meets Airport Road, offers day-long or extended tours in motorboats and sea kayaks throughout Sandwich Bay and the closer reaches of the Labrador Sea, including to destinations like the resettled communities at Pack's Harbour and Dove Brook. Experience Labrador also organizes fishing trips to various rivers and brings hikers along the wild and beautiful Wonderstrand beaches to the north.

Accommodations and Food

Cartwright has the **Northside Hotel** (Main Road, 709/938-7122, $120), located downtown within walking distance of both community wharves and all the main stores, restaurants, services, and sights. Northside has six rooms, each with a private entrance, as well as a pub on the premises.

The **Cartwright Hotel** (Airport Road, 709/938-7414, www.cartwrighthotel.ca, $120) is outside of town about halfway to the local gravel airstrip. It has 10 rooms, a licensed lounge, and a restaurant that specializes in in-season Labrador cuisine.

Cartwright also has **Brenda's Bed and Breakfast** (709/938-7938, $60) in the original Grenfell nurses residence converted for holiday use.

Services

There is a detachment of the **Royal Canadian Mounted Police** (709/938-7218) in Cartwright. There is also a branch of the **Labrador-Grenfell Health Corporation** (709/938-7285). The local **Eagle River Credit Union** (1 Back Road, 709/938-7468) has a branch in Cartwright as well.

Getting There

Cartwright is 200 kilometers north of Port Hope Simpson on Route 510. In total, it's 338 kilometers from Red Bay—a very long unpaved drive.

ISLAND OF PONDS

For an experience of Labrador that's far outside the usual tourist track, the remote Island of Ponds can be reached from Cartwright on board MV *Northern Ranger,* a ferry run by Labrador Marine (709/535-0810, www.tw.gov.nl.ca), which carries passengers and freight once a week in the summer to dock at Black Tickle.

Black Tickle and its smaller neighbour **Domino** are the only two communities on the 12-kilometer-long Island of Ponds that sits out in the Labrador Sea about halfway south to Charlottetown. People settled on this beautiful, but stark island almost 200 years ago to make a living from the sea, and they are proud to remain there still today, despite the hardships they face. There are no hotels or official B&Bs in either Black Tickle or Domino, but visitors can sometimes arrange accommodations with local homeowners. The provincial government maintains a gravel airstrip on Island of Ponds about two kilometers from Black Tickle, serviced by Air Labrador (800/563-3042, www.airlabrador.com).

MEALY MOUNTAINS

Northwest of Cartwright, the wild Mealy Mountains, home to a rare herd of woodland caribou, are in the process of becoming a national park reserve. Once established, the **Mealy Mountain National Park Reserve** will stretch from the Atlantic Ocean to central Labrador and encompass not only the Mealy Mountains themselves, but also several thousand square kilometers of forest, bogland, rivers, and lakes. It also will include the world-famous Wonderstrands: These beautiful 40-kilometer-long sandy beaches were known and named by Norse Vikings more than 1,000 years ago (known today as the Porcupine Strands).

Currently this area is completely road-free—and is intended to remain so—but it is accessible by water and by air and, in the wintertime, by snowmobile.

◖ EAGLE RIVER

The Eagle and other rivers that flow out of the Mealy Mountain Park are renowned for their record-breaking trout and salmon, and they attract anglers from all over the world. The future **Eagle River Provincial Waterway Park** and is intended to protect most of the Eagle River system, starting at the mouth but not quite taking in all of the headwaters. This park will also be completely road-free and accessible by water and by air and, in the wintertime, by snowmobile.

The most lucrative sports activity in southern Labrador is undoubtedly fly-fishing for Atlantic salmon. Dedicated anglers—including famous Hollywood actors and former American presidents—come from all over the world to wade into Labrador's cold and clean rivers to try to hook one of the many record-breaking fish that live in them. Most camps and lodges are fly-in only by small fixed-wing aircraft or helicopter.

Fishing Lodges

At the headwaters of the Eagle River, **Park Lake Lodge** (709/896-3301, www.parklakelodge.com, $500) is one of the oldest in Labrador and is on an island in a lake that teems with salmon and trout. At least one guide has more than 20 years experience taking anglers around Park Lake and into the upper Eagle River.

However, he's only one of several experienced native and non-native guides employed by Park Lake Lodge, which is owned and managed by the development corporation of the Labrador Innu. Good meals are provided, but accommodations are spartan and guests must often arrange their own transportation to and from the lake.

Rifflin' Hitch Lodge (709/640-2414, www.rifflinhitchlodge.com, $3,000) is located about halfway down the Eagle River and can only be reached by helicopter—one of which the lodge owns for the convenience of its guests. For the $3,000 charged per night (with a three-night minimum stay), Rifflin' Hitch offers gourmet meals, near-luxurious accommodations in an impressively beautiful log-built lodge, and guided fly-fishing in several nearby rapids and pools.

For more options, lodges and outfitters operating on the Eagle River include **Eagle River Trout Lodge** (709/543-2274, http://flyfishinglabrador.com), **Labrador Sportsfish Ltd.** (709/896-2421, http://woodwards.nf.ca/Eagles Nest/Eagles_Nst.html), and **Cloud 9 Salmon Lodge** (709/938-7128, www.cloud9salmonlodge.com).

Happy Valley-Goose Bay and Vicinity

Today it's called Happy Valley-Goose Bay, but before the Second World War, before the Canadian military built one of the largest airfields in North America on this wide sandy plateau at the western end of Hamilton Inlet, it was known to the families all around as Uncle Bob's Berry Patch. After the base was built it soon became Labrador's biggest employer and Goose Bay (it wasn't to amalgamate with Happy Valley until the 1980s) quickly became the region's biggest town—as it remains, with some competition from Labrador City.

SIGHTS

The Goose Bay Airbase was built in World War II as a staging point to ship Allied airplanes, equipment, and personnel to Europe. Although military interest in Happy Valley-Goose Bay has waned of late, for all of World War II and most of the decades afterwards, the base was heavily used for training and overseas deployment not only by Canada, but also by the air forces of the United States, France, Germany, Great Britain, and other NATO countries.

Much of that history can be seen at the official **Labrador Military Museum** (Building 295, 5 Wing Goose Bay, 709/896-5212 or 709/896-1444, Thurs.–Tues. in summer, by appointment rest of the year). Artifacts on display include relics from plane crashes and Cold War radio equipment. Located at 5 Wing Goose Bay air base, the museum also features

LABRADOR

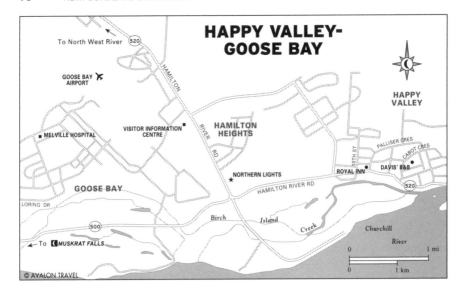

memorials to fallen soldiers—most notably two officers who lost their lives on a rescue mission in 2002.

An unofficial private military museum can be found off the base and down in Happy Valley—downstairs in the store **Northern Lights** (170 Hamilton River Road, 709/896-5939). The owner of the store has spent several decades collecting local and non-local military and war artifacts and set aside a room in his shop (which sells clothing, camping gear, army surplus, artwork, souvenirs, and spice grinders) to put them on free public display. Artifacts include uniforms, decorations, old photos, a jet plane's ejection seat, and a rusted antique mortar cannon.

To see something of how the Goose Bay airbase used to look in its very earliest days—and maybe even catch a glimpse of a ghost or two—take a drive to the north side of town on Hamilton River Road. Before you descend the hill to the Terrington Basin docks, turn left into the **Canadian Side** to see wartime buildings that have stood since the 1940s. Not all of the buildings of the original Canadian base have survived, but enough have stood the test of years to give some idea of how the area

looked when it swarmed with Allied airmen. The first control tower can be seen near the current runways, where it is attached to one of three surviving aircraft hangers. Six of the once numerous H-block barracks still stand in varying degrees of repair and renovation, as do several other structures, including the wartime map building and the official harbourmaster's residence. The old Canadian Side can be toured without restriction, but unfortunately none of the historic buildings are open to the public.

There's one more stop for the military-minded—and flight enthusiasts—in Happy Valley-Goose Bay. On a wide plot of grassy ground in front of the civilian air terminal, the base has assembled a sizable collection of historic decommissioned aircraft, including a British Vulcan bomber. There's also a Cold War-era radar dish on display.

SPORTS AND RECREATION
Skiing

Whatever the season, a good place to head in central Labrador is to the **Birch Brook Nordic Ski Club** (Route 520 east of Gosling Lake, 709/896-2718, www.birchbrook.ca).

Birch Brook has more than 30 kilometers of backcountry trails suitable for hiking in the summer and groomed for snowshoeing and cross-country skiing in the winter. It has a brand new log chalet for social functions and a remote lakeside cabin for overnight stays. Skiing season is usually November–April, depending on snow conditions. A single day pass costs $10, and equipment rentals are available for an extra charge. Advanced bookings are required for the overnight shelter.

Hunting and Fishing

In addition to those serving the Eagle River, several hunting and fishing lodges and outfitters operate out of Happy Valley-Goose Bay, including **Labrador Wildlife Expeditions** (709/896-2037, www.labradorhuntingfishing.com), **Coopers' Minipi Camps** (877/266-7377, http://minipicamps.com), and **Double Mer Fishing Camp** (709/896-3115).

ENTERTAINMENT AND EVENTS
Performing Arts

For a variety of entertainment events, with something new scheduled just about every week, check out the brand new state-of-the-art **O'Brien Arts Centre** (Churchill Street, 709/896-4028 box office or 709/896-4027 general, www.obrienartscentre.ca, 9 A.M.–5 P.M. Mon.–Fri. and at one hour before showtime), a 300-seat theatre attached to Happy Valley-Goose Bay's Mealy Mountain Collegiate school. The Arts Centre is worth visiting just to see the large student-made clay mural that decorates the lobby.

Festivals

The year's festivals and events start in March with the eight-day **Sno-Break** (709/896-3489, www.snobreak.ca). The event is a celebration of the region's most-loved (and sometimes most hated) resources: snow and ice. It includes skating, skiing, curling, snow sculpturing, community lunches, snowmobile tours, and snowmobile races.

Later in March, the annual 40-kilometer cross-country ski race called the **Big Land Loppet** (709/896-2718, www.birchbrook.ca) is run up the South Branch Road from the TransLabrador Highway to 5 Wing Goose Bay.

On a weekend at the end of July the **Labrador Canoe Regatta** (www.canoelabrador.ca) is held on Gosling Lake, bringing teams from all over the region to race against each other in large painted war canoes. The Regatta is organized on the beach in Gosling Park, where concession stands are set up and, for a fee, unserviced lots are made available for pitching tents and parking recreational vehicles. The event includes live music and the annual Labrador Strongman Competition.

Happy Valley-Goose Bay puts on the **Big Land Fair** (E.J. Broomfield Arena, 2 Churchill Street, 709/896-8506, cbest@cledb.ca, www.explorelabrador.nf.ca) in the second week of September. The fall fair is the time and place for local farmers to display their produce, local craftspeople to sell their artwork, and local musicians to flaunt their talents.

A fairly new event in central Labrador that is rapidly growing in popularity is the annual **Trapline Marathon** (709/896-3000, www.traplinemarathon.ca), held around the second week of October. This meticulously planned and executed competition has quickly become a qualifying run for the Boston Marathon. Runners have the choice of tackling the full marathon from North West River, the half-marathon from the Birch Brook Nordic Ski Club, or the 10-kilometers from the Otter Creek floatplane base. All three competitions are held simultaneously, and they follow Route 520 into Happy Valley-Goose Bay and then Hamilton River Road down to the finish line at the Kinsmen Park.

ACCOMMODATIONS AND FOOD

Perhaps the most comfortable accommodations in town, but not necessarily the most expensive, are provided by the **Cherrywood Corporate Suites** (5 Cherrywood Drive, 709/896-4000, www.cherrywoodsuites.ca,

LABRADOR

$109–149, weekly and monthly rates available), just outside the main gates of 5 Wing Goose Bay. The Cherrywood offers six large suites that include fully equipped kitchens. There's also an outdoor barbecue deck and free laundry facilities.

Hotel North One (25 Loring Drive, 709/896-9301 or 877/996-9301, www.atyp. com/hotelnorth, $139 rooms, $189 suites) has 54 rooms, the Mariners Galley Steak and Seafood Restaurant, and a business centre with free wireless internet. The related **Hotel North Two** (382 Hamilton River Road, 709/896-3398 or 888/892-5505, www.hotelnorthtwo.ca, $139 rooms, $189 suites) has 40 rooms and a Jungle Jim's Restaurant.

Also at the corner of Loring Drive is the 66-room **Labrador Inn** (380 Hamilton River Road, 800/563-2763, www.labradorinn.nf.ca, $84–135 rooms, $115–150 mini-suites, $175 VIP suite). There are rooms and suites available, as well as the on-site Don Cherry's Bar and Grill.

TMT's Bed and Breakfast (451 Hamilton River Road, 709/896-4404, $45–65) is on Hamilton River Road east of Loring Drive by the residential area called Spruce Park. Open year-round, TMT's has six rooms that share full kitchen facilities and are completely separate from the family residence.

The **Royal Inn** (3 Royal Avenue, 888/440-2456, www.royalinnandsuites.ca, $79–139) in the Happy Valley part of town has 16 rooms and 21 suites. A continental breakfast is included in the price, and a valet service is available.

Also in Happy Valley is the four-room **Al-Ving Hotel** (6 Grand Street, 709/896-7331, $65), which offers home-cooked meals in the attached Lavenia's Country Kitchen.

Davis' Bed and Breakfast (14 Cabot Crescent, 709/896-5077, www.bbcanada.com/davisbb, $60–80) in the valley has four government-inspected rooms, each with private bathrooms. Davis' is not open December–April.

Outside of the main townsite, but still within the town boundaries about 15 kilometers east on Route 520, are the **Goose River Lodges** (Route 520, 709/896-2600, www.

gooseriverlodges.ca, $107.35 for up to four). Nine two-bedroom cottages are available—one of which is wheelchair accessible—all with fully equipped kitchens. "Everything is provided except the food." The lodge also has 16 RV sites, 12 of which are fully serviced.

SERVICES

There is a detachment of the **Royal Canadian Mounted Police** (149 Hamilton River Road, 709/896-3383) in Happy Valley-Goose Bay. Labrador-Grenfell Health Corporation runs the **Labrador Health Centre Hospital** (Hamilton River Road, 709/897-2000 general switchboard, 709/897-2399 emergency ward, 709/896-2100 to call an ambulance) in the lower end of Happy Valley-Goose Bay.

GETTING THERE
By Air

The easiest and quickest way to get into Happy Valley-Goose Bay—but not necessarily the least expensive—is by flying. The main airline hub for the entire Labrador region is the **Goose Bay Airport** (Goose Bay Airport Corporation, 709/896-6668, www.goosebayairport.com), the small civilian air terminal currently undergoing extensive renovations on 5 Wing Goose Bay. Several carriers, such as Air Canada, Air Labrador, and Provincial Airlines, regularly fly into Goose Bay from St. John's, Gander, Deer Lake, and Halifax, connecting to further Labrador destinations in all directions. Unlike other military bases in Canada, 5 Wing Goose Bay is open to the public and there is no restriction on access to the airport or to other services on the base.

By Car

Coming from the east is Labrador's newest highway, a gravel track that runs for more than 300 unserviced kilometers between Port Hope Simpson and Happy Valley-Goose Bay.

SHESHATSHIU AND MUD LAKE

Across the mouth of the Churchill River from each other, neither Sheshatshiu nor Mud Lake offer much in the way of tourism attractions,

winter at the Mud Lake School

but both are unique and often beautiful communities that are worth visiting in their own right.

Sheshatshiu

Sheshatshiu is the largest of the two Innu reserves in Labrador, with a rapidly growing population of 1,200 people or more. As capital of the Innu Nation, Sheshatshiu has experienced a building boom in recent years and has come out of it with several superb examples of beautifully designed public buildings, including the offices of the Innu Nation and the Sheshatshiu Innu First Nation, the new Innu School on Top Road, as well as the **RCMP detachment** (beside Route 520, 709/497-8700 or 800/709-7267) and the **Mani Ashini Health Clinic** (709/497-8202 or 709/497-8331) near the bridge by Route 500.

Mud Lake

The old and tiny village of Mud Lake is difficult to reach, located as it is on the south side of the Churchill River with no bridges or roads

leading to it from anywhere, but that isolation gives the community a charm that few others can boast. The historic settlement, which happened to have been instrumental in setting the border between Labrador and Quebec, is a pretty collection of small wooden houses linked only by trails and set amidst trees beside watery channels—a small Venice of the North, one might call it. Aside from around two weeks in the fall and another two in the spring (during freeze-up of the Churchill River and its subsequent break-up) when Mud Lake can only be reached by helicopter, private transportation by boat or snowmobile across the river can be arranged at Buck's Landing, downstream of Happy Valley-Goose Bay at the end of Mud Lake Road.

NORTH WEST RIVER

North West River is a vibrant and historic community 40 kilometers east of Happy Valley-Goose Bay along the north shore of Lake Melville.

© MICHAEL JOHANSEN

kayaking past the Hudson's Bay Company trading post built in North West River in 1927

Sights

Before a bridge was built in the 1970s to link the hitherto roadless community of North West River to Route 520 (the 33-kilometer highway to Happy Valley-Goose Bay), the main way residents and visitors traveled across the deep channel to Sheshatshiu was on board a small red-and-white striped cable car that's now mounted on display by North West River's historic waterfront.

The bright **cable car** can easily be seen from the bridge as one enters North West River, and it makes an ideal landmark. Most of the community's history took place all around the spot it sits—the stony beach having known the passage of countless people and boats for hundreds and even thousands of years.

That history can be seen nearby in the **Labrador Heritage Society Museum** (3 River Road, 709/497-8282, www.townofnwr. ca, 9:30 A.M.–5:30 P.M. daily June–Oct., $2 adults, $1 children), which has been established in what was originally built as a Hudson's Bay Company trading post in the 1920s. The museum holds artifacts from the community's fishing and trapping past, as well as remnants of the ill-fated 1902 Hubbard Expedition and many other items.

North West River actually boasts two museums. The second is at a high point in town: The **Labrador Interpretation Centre** (2 Portage Road, 709/497-8566, www.therooms. ca/museum/labrador_interpretation.asp, hours vary by season, open year-round, free) was built to display and teach the history of the entire region and the cultures of the people who live in Labrador. The centre has three permanent displays set up by the region's three aboriginal groups, the Innu, the Inuit, and the Metis. There's also space available for touring exhibitions, and a small theatre suitable for demonstrations and for the performing arts. No admission fee is charged, but donations are welcome.

If you're in North West River (and it's a nice clear day or a bright moon-filled night), you can't leave town without having a look at the view from **Sunday Hill,** which can be found by following Sunday Hill Road a short distance northwards until you can't go any higher. Sunday Hill has been fitted with two benched platforms that provide breathtaking views westwards towards Grand Lake, northwards towards the prominent historic landmark called Mokami Hill, and eastwards over Lake Melville and the Mealy Mountains.

Festivals

In July, North West River holds the popular **'Striver Beach Festival** (Lester Burry Memorial Park, 709/497-8228, www.nwrbeachfestival.com), which features almost three days of live music played by local and out-of-town artists on the permanent stage in the Lester Burry Memorial Park on the town's riverside waterfront. The many concerts by local musicians and at least one big headliner are free, and there are plenty of other attractions in addition to the music, including food of all kinds and closing-night fireworks.

Getting There

The 33-kilometer Route 520 joins North West River to Happy Valley-Goose Bay.

WATERFALLS

Lovers of scenic waterfalls have several they can visit in central Labrador, the foremost of these being Muskrat Falls.

Simeon Falls

Small, but the quickest to find, Simeon Falls lies beside an ancient Innu travel route and several berry-picking grounds. Just off Route 520 between Happy Valley-Goose Bay and North West River, this waterfall is in some quiet spruce woods, just beyond the monument that marks the boundary of Happy Valley-Goose Bay. There's space to park in a short lay-by on the far side of the road, and the path to follow is marked with a sign that announces, Scenic Waterfall. The short path takes about 15 minutes to walk, and it's usable all year, although the falls are often frozen nearly solid for much of the winter.

pathway to Simeon Falls

© MICHAEL JOHANSEN

LABRADOR

(Muskrat Falls

Muskrat Falls is a massive two-stepped torrent created where the wide waters of the Churchill River get channeled into a narrow gorge around a high rocky knoll called Manitu-utshu—a sacred site of the Labrador Innu who believe a powerful entity lives on the hill above the falls.

Muskrat Falls is located less than 40 kilometers west of Happy Valley-Goose Bay on Route 500. A dirt lane leads for about three kilometers from the highway to several uncontrolled parking areas and campsites, one of which provides a view eastwards over the swirling downstream basin. A footpath leads from the parking areas down a steep hill to the edge of the upper falls and can be followed alongside the riverbank to the flat rocks by the lower drop—a total distance of about four kilometers over very rough terrain.

Traverspine River

Not too far away—another 30 kilometers from Route 500—the new gravel highway to southern Labrador crosses the Traverspine River close above a series of overlapping falls that really shouldn't be missed—and, given the newness of the road, it's one that not many people have yet seen for themselves. The river crossing is unmarked, and there is no place to park except on the side of the road, but the falls are close by and can be approached by a path that crosses a cleared area to cliffs beside the top of the high cascades. The path eventually descends into the gorge.

Western Labrador

Western Labrador was a sparsely inhabited, trackless wilderness only 50 years ago, but today it's home to more than 1,000 people in two communities and is beyond a doubt the most prosperous area in the region.

LABRADOR CITY AND WABUSH

Twin cities of sorts, both Wabush and Labrador City started life as company mining towns back in the 1950s and they're both still dependent on miners digging iron ore out of the ground.

Sights

Because of the economic importance of mining to the area, it might not be surprising that the two most popular tourist attractions are **Wabush Mines** (709/285-7100) and the **Iron Ore Company of Canada** mines (709/944-8400). Tours of both facilities can be arranged by calling the respective company.

Lovers of fine art should pay a visit to the **Labrador City town council office** (317 Hudson Drive, Labrador City, 709/944-2621, www.labradorwest.com) and ask politely (if the room is not already open for a public meeting) if you can go into the council chambers to have a look at what's hanging on the walls. When the Iron Ore Company set up its first camp at Carol Lake and started digging for iron more than 50 years ago, it commissioned Group of Seven painter A.Y. Jackson and others to document the work in art. Three of those paintings—one by Jackson himself—were given to the municipal government, and they now grace the public council chambers.

Sports and Recreation

If you like stretching your legs, do like the locals do and follow the popular **Jean Lake Walking Trail** (709/282-3142 Wabush Recreation Centre) that circles a large pond beside Wabush for a distance of about five kilometers. It's the quickest way to see a small but lush slice of natural Labrador and gives a view of the town you wouldn't otherwise see. The trailhead is found on Grenfell Drive in Wabush.

Avid snowmobilers can find their way into the vast wilderness of the Ungava Peninsula on the more than 500 kilometers of professionally groomed trails maintained by the **White Wolf Snowmobile Club** (office: Hayden-Powell Avenue, Labrador City, 709/944-7401 membership, www.white-wolf.net). The club has built chalets equipped with woodstoves in convenient locations around the trail system and has a clubhouse available for social activities.

Sport hunting of caribou is being curtailed in Labrador because of conservation concerns, but several outfitters and lodges still operate out of western Labrador and offer **fishing and hunting excursions** into the interior. Among them are Blue Mountain Outfitters (746 Stirling Crescent, Labrador City, 709/640-2085, http://bluemountainhunting.com), Northern Lights Lodge (Labrador City, 709-944-7475, www.labradorfrontier.com), Labrador Caribou Outfitting (4036 Duley Crescent, Labrador City, 709/944-6315, www.labradorcaribououtfitters.com), and Labrador Adventures and Outfitting (Wabush, 709/282-5369, www.caribouhunts.ca).

Festivals and Events

In March, Labrador City puts on the **Labrador**

Winter Carnival (709/944-3602, www.labradorwest.com), a weekend of skiing, sliding, dogsledding, snowmobiling and bonfires.

Near the end of winter in the month of May—a season called 'spring' everywhere else—the town council of Labrador City organizes an annual **Polar Bear Dip** (www.labradorwest.com). Residents and visitors alike are welcome to strip down to their swim trunks and brave swimming in Labrador's icy-cold water.

Accommodations and Food

If you're looking for an inexpensive, but homelike place to stay—and you don't mind sharing a bathroom—the **Twin Cities Bed and Breakfast** (325 Viking Crescent, Labrador City, 709/944-2875, $60) fits the bill. Proprietor Lottie Baggs says all guests are free to make themselves at home.

PJ's Inn by the Lake (606 Tamarack Drive, Labrador City, 888/944-6648, www.pjsinnbythelake.com, $110–140) is open year-round and has five available rooms. Four of the rooms overlook Little Wabush Lake.

The **Carol Inn** (215 Drake Avenue, Labrador City, 888/799-7736, www.carolinn.com, $121) has 21 rooms that are all fitted with fridges, stoves, microwave ovens, and other necessary utensils.

Located right by the main traffic lights on Route 500, the 54-room **Two Seasons Inn** (Avalon Drive, Labrador City, 800/670-7667, www.twoseasonsinn.com, $134) has an exercise room and a lounge and advertises that its dining room serves French cuisine.

The 68-room **Wabush Hotel** (9 Grenfell Drive, Wabush, 709/282-3221, www.wabushhotel.com, $100 single) is impossible to miss, since it's one of the largest buildings in Wabush and it looks like it actually belongs in the Swiss Alps. Anyone driving over the TransLabrador Highway gets a 10-per-cent discount. The Great Wall Restaurant and the Great Echo Bar are both on the premises.

Information and Services

Whether you're coming into Lab West through the airport, or by road out of Quebec, a good

warning sign on the new TransLabrador Highway

© MICHAEL JOHANSEN

first stop is the **Gateway Labrador Centre** (Route 500, Labrador City, 709/944-5399, www.gatewaylabrador.ca, 9 A.M.–9 P.M. daily mid-June–August, reduced hours rest of the year), located between the Labrador Mall to the west and the Royal Newfoundland Constabulary detachment to the east. Staff at Gateway Labrador offer tourist information and can act as guides to the exhibits of cultural artifacts and displays that trace Labrador's long and colourful history.

For police services, there is a detachment of the **Royal Newfoundland Constabulary** (Booth Ave., 709/944-7602) in Labrador City. Labrador-Grenfell Health Corporation provides health services; reach them at **Captain William Jackman Memorial Hospital** (709/944-2632).

Getting There
Aside from Goose Bay, **Wabush Airport** (709/282-5412, www.tc.gc.ca) is the next largest airport in the region and serves all of western Labrador (as well as parts of the province of Quebec). It is a destination for flights coming from Montreal, Quebec City, and Sept-Iles, as well as from Happy Valley-Goose Bay. The Wabush Airport is located near Route 500 on the way into Wabush.

People traveling to western Labrador by car must be prepared for hundreds of kilometers of often poorly maintained gravel roads. Travelers can drive north to western Labrador from Baie-Comeau through Quebec on Route 389, which is a 500-kilometer prospect (half of it paved). Services and accommodations can be found near the Manic 5 hydro dam and 100 kilometers north of it, but otherwise there's nothing until they get to the town of Fermont, which is located right beside the Labrador border.

Route 500, the so-called TransLabrador Highway or Freedom Road, runs for more than 500 kilometers between Wabush and Happy Valley-Goose Bay. It is in the process of being paved but is still mostly surfaced with loose gravel. Services, including fuel and accommodations, can be found at around the half-way point at Churchill Falls.

MENIHEK NORDIC SKI CLUB
By far the premier winter sports facility in Labrador is the Menihek Nordic Ski Club (Smokey Mountain Road, 709/944-5842, www.meniheknordicski.com, 9 A.M.–5 P.M. daily Nov.–Apr., depending on snow conditions, $15 per day), located outside Labrador City on Smokey Mountain Road past Beverly Lake. Menihek has a total of 34 kilometers of groomed trails, three kilometers of which are lighted for nighttime skiing. The trails are designed both for recreation and for world-class competition. The grounds also includes a biathlon range.

Right across Smokey Mountain Road is the **Smokey Mountain Ski Lodge** (709/944-2129, www.smokeymountain.ca), which caters to alpine skiers and snowboarders.

Festivals and Events
The **Labrador Open Cross Country Ski Races** take place in early December and feature 10-kilometer free ski and traditional races, as well as the Labrador Snow Training Camp. The races are sanctioned by Cross Country Canada and are hosted by the Menihek Nordic Ski Club.

In March, Menihek holds another cross-country ski race: the **Great Labrador Loppet.** Racers have a choice between a 10-kilometer, a 27-kilometer, and a 54-kilometer groomed course that runs between Labrador City and Fermont, Quebec.

CHURCHILL FALLS
Built as a company town in the 1970s and remains so today, Churchill Falls is home of a huge underground hydroelectric generating station.

Sights
Tours of the hydroelectric generating station can be arranged by through **Churchill Falls (Labrador) Corporation** (709/925-3335). This huge powerhouse in the heart of the wilderness taps the currents of Labrador's largest watershed to keep the lights shining in homes all across Quebec and into the United States. The

© MICHAEL JOHANSEN

the giant transmission towers of Churchill Falls

tours starts off with an orientation session and a fitting for a hardhat in one of the administration buildings before the group is driven to the actual site.

Visitors to this town shouldn't miss the chance to see the reason this massive hydroelectric generator was built in the middle of Labrador's vast wilderness: the **Churchill Falls** themselves. Once called Grand Falls (just as the Churchill River was once called the Grand River) until the government of Newfoundland changed the name to honour the British wartime Prime Minister Sir Winston Churchill, the stream that now

lightly cascades down the high smooth cliff west of town is only a trickle compared to what it used to be. Before its waters were diverted to spin huge electrical turbines, the roar of Grand Falls could be heard miles away, and the very ground shook all around it. To obtain a good view over the falls and the deep gorge beneath them, follow a marked footpath that leads south from a parking lot on the west side of the one-lane steel bridge that crosses the Churchill River about 20 kilometers from the town on Route 500.

Accommodations

Churchill Falls has two places to stay.

The **Churchill Falls Inn** (800/229-3269, $115 single) is located in the main shopping and recreation complex in the middle of town and features a large restaurant.

The **Black Spruce Lodge** (709/925-3233, $85) has eight rooms that share kitchen facilities and a large television lounge. Arrange accommodations by phone or with a visit to Strickland's Auto and Gas on John Cabot Drive.

Services

For police services, there is a detachment of the **Royal Newfoundland Constabulary** (709/925-3524) in Churchill Falls' central complex. **Labrador-Grenfell Health Corporation** (709/925-3381) provides health services.

Getting There

Churchill Falls is located at about the halfway point of the more than 500-kilometer distance between Happy Valley-Goose Bay and Wabush.

LABRADOR

Northern Labrador

With no roads going there, northern Labrador is about as remote as it gets. For more than 200 years, travelers have usually approached the six northern communities from the south, following the increasingly barren coastline north on the ocean waves or the frozen sea.

Getting There

No roads have yet been built to any of the six communities on Labrador's north coast, namely Rigolet, Makkovik, Postville, Hopedale, Natuashish, and Nain. All are served by government-maintained gravel airstrips that can only take short-range propeller aircraft, such as those flown by Air Labrador and Provincial Airways.

The MV *Northern Ranger,* operated by **Labrador Marine** (866/535-2567, www.labradormarine.com), carries freight and passengers out of Happy Valley-Goose Bay to the six communities on the north coast and back again once a week, usually June–November, depending on seasonal ice conditions. Rates vary depending on destination and onboard accommodations, but they're certainly competitive with the cost of flying. Cabins and meals are available on board, as is entertainment in a licensed lounge. The ferry is heavily used by local travelers, so visitors are strongly advised to make reservations as early as possible.

In the wintertime the Labrador Sea is usually frozen solid, so you can go by snowmachine if you know the way or have a local guide (be prepared for overnight camping in temperatures that can drop far below minus 40 degrees Celsius).

RIGOLET

Rigolet (709/947-3382, Inuit Community Government), which happens to be the southernmost Inuit settlement in the world, is the first community along the way, only a six-hour sail from Happy Valley-Goose Bay. Built as it is beside the narrow but deep channel that connects the 150-kilometer-long Hamilton Inlet with Groswater Bay, Rigolet is not only a crossroads for the people of central and coastal Labrador, but also for the myriad creatures of the sea. Millions of fish migrate back and forth through the tidal channel, attracting thousands of seals that calve on Lake Melville's ice and dozens of whales that feed and breach within sight of the town—sometimes only meters from shore—giving residents and visitors alike hours of opportunity to film them, photograph them, or just enjoy the extraordinary sight of them.

The Hudson's Bay Company set up a trading post in Rigolet in 1834, but while none of their very first buildings remain, the **HBC Net Loft**—constructed for use by local salmon fishermen in the 1870s—has survived the years and been restored for use as a museum. Plans are in the works to restore and reconstruct other historic buildings, and the municipal government has almost finished laying down what will be the second-longest boardwalk in the world. Only the boardwalk in Atlantic City, New Jersey, will be longer.

Accommodations

Rigolet, unfortunately, no longer has a hotel. Accommodations may possibly be arranged in private homes.

Services

The **Royal Canadian Mounted Police** (709/947-3400) maintains a detachment office in Rigolet. **Labrador-Grenfell Health Corporation** (709/947-3386) also has a nursing station here.

MAKKOVIK

The next stop north is Makkovik (709/923-2221 Inuit Community Government), which was the southernmost settlement established in Labrador by German missionaries from the Moravian Church more than 250 years ago. This town was actually the Moravians' second attempt to found a mission in Makkovik Bay, and the foundations of the original abandoned site were recently discovered in nearby Ford's

© MICHAEL JOHANSEN

Rigolet boardwalk

Bight, a short boatride from the modern community. Current archaeological digs are open for public viewing by arrangement.

One of the mission buildings the Moravians eventually constructed in Makkovik now houses the quaintly named **White Elephant Museum** (709/923-2425, www.labradorvirtualmuseum.ca/wem, July and Aug.), which tells the history of the community in large part with a display of antique cultural artifacts—the kind of things that might have ended up in a 'white elephant' sale had the guardians of Makkovik's heritage not been as vigilant as they were.

About 15 kilometers north of the community on Cape Makkovik, the remains of the early Cold War-era can be found. **Pinetree Line** is a radar base where American soldiers once scanned the skies for attacking Soviet nuclear bombers. Today only the foundations sit on one of the highest points on the cape.

Accommodations

Makkovik has two places to stay: the five-room **Adlavik Inn** (709/923-2389, www.labradorabletours.com) and **David's B&B** (709/923-2430).

Services

Labrador-Grenfell Health Corporation (709/923-2229) has a nursing station in Makkovik.

POSTVILLE

Postville (709/479-8300 Inuit Community Government) is actually to the south and west of Makkovik, but it's third on the ferry's north-bound route since all boats must round Cape Makkovik before entering long Kaipokok Bay. Although Postville was founded in the early 1800s as a trading post (hence the name), none of the original buildings remain. However, the town does boast Labrador's oldest **Pentacostal Church** (709/479-9871).

Accommodations

Postville has the **Postville Hotel** (709/479-9881) and **North Coast Hospitality** (709/479-9766).

Services
Labrador-Grenfell Health Corporation (709/479-9851) has a nursing station in Postville.

HOPEDALE
Of all the communities on Labrador's north coast, Hopedale (709/933-3864) has been the most successful in preserving and restoring the historic and cultural legacy left to the people by the early Moravian missionaries. The church, a dormitory, an ammunition building, and the Dead House (the old mission morgue) still stand on the Hopedale waterfront. These were all built in Germany almost 200 years ago, taken apart, sailed across the ocean, and reassembled on a windswept rocky point in the Labrador Sea. All the mission buildings have been restored and are being maintained in as near their original condition as possible. The church is still being used for worship, but the dormitory—once the home of religious brothers from Europe—has been converted into a museum that displays a large and fascinating collection of local and regional artifacts that date from prehistoric times to more recent years.

Accommodations
In Hopedale, there's the **Amaguk Inn** (709/933-3750).

Services
The **Royal Canadian Mounted Police** (709/933-3820) maintains a detachment office in Hopedale. **Labrador-Grenfell Health Corporation** (709/933-3857) also has a nursing station here.

NATUASHISH
Natuashish is the youngest community in the province, having only been founded in 2002, but it boasts a culture that's as old as the hills and sea around it. The Mushuau Innu—the local aboriginal people who are closely related to the Sheshatshiu Innu—had their community relocated twice in the last century, after they were encouraged to give up their nomadic lives and settle in one spot. Both of the first

two settlements are now ghost towns that can be reached within several hours by boat or snowmobile from the modern townsite. The older of the two, Old Davis Inlet as it came to be called when a new Davis Inlet was built in the 1960s, still has a house and a trading post that dates back to the 1920s. Both structures are in an advanced state of disrepair, approaching collapse.

Natuashish (709/478-8827, Mushuau Innu First Nation), on the other hand, is brand new and a good place to learn about the vibrant culture of the Barrenland Innu.

Services
The **Royal Canadian Mounted Police** (709/478-8900) maintains a detachment office in Natuashish. **Labrador-Grenfell Health Corporation** (709/478-8842) also has a nursing station here.

NAIN
Nain (709/922-2842 Inuit Community Government) is Newfoundland and Labrador's northernmost inhabited community and, with more than 1,200 inhabitants, it's the largest on the north coast. Moravians settled Nain in 1771, but unfortunately none of the original buildings remain. Tragically, the last surviving mission building, which was being used as a museum, was destroyed only in a fire that caused the loss of countless priceless Inuit and Moravian artifacts. However, an early 20th-century Moravian Church with a unique steeple still stands overlooking the town's main docks and is used today for worship, weddings, and funerals.

Nain is also the staging point for trips farther north up the coast. The most popular destinations are the abandoned but restored Moravian Mission at Hebron and the new Torngat Mountains National Park Reserve. No scheduled transportation services operate north of Nain, but private boat charters can be arranged with local people.

Accommodations
The **Atsanik Lodge** (709/922-2910) is available for people staying overnight in Nain.

Services

The **Royal Canadian Mounted Police** (709/922-2862) maintains a detachment office in Nain. **Labrador-Grenfell Health Corporation** (709/922-2912) also has a nursing station here.

HEBRON

Hebron was the site of a Moravian mission established in the early 1800s, but it was forcibly abandoned in 1959. The original church—a unique structure that was prefabricated in Europe and reassembled in Labrador—has been saved from collapse and restored to something close to its original state. While Hebron has not yet been resettled, one family acts as caretakers of the historic site. Hebron is administered by the **Nunatsiavut Government** (709/922-2942) in Nain.

◖ TORNGAT MOUNTAINS NATIONAL PARK

The Torngat Mountains National Park Reserve (709/922-1290, www.parkscanada.gc.ca/torngat) protects all of mainland Labrador north of Saglek Bay and is the newest national park in Canada. The Torngats are pure wilderness: remote, pristine, and dangerous. Majestic polar bears rule a bleak landscape of ice and rock, and the mountains rise straight out of the sea and steal the breath of anyone who sees them. Getting there takes several hours by plane and several days by boat. Tourists are strongly advised to hire local guides before visiting the park.

LABRADOR

Index

A

Admiralty House Museum and Archives: 18
Appalachian Trail: 62
aquariums: 51
Arches Provincial Park: 52
Argentia Sunset Park: 28
arts and crafts: Big Land Fair 79; Glenn John Arts and Craft Centre 46; Heritage Research Centre 68; Labrador Culture Craft Shop 69; Labrador Straits Museum 68; Mi'kmaq Craft Shop 46; Mikmaw Discovery Centre 46; Provincial Art Gallery 15
Avalon Peninsula: 25-30
aviation: 39, 77-78

B

backpacking: 62
Bakeapple Folk Festival: 67
Bannerman Park: 15
Basque whalers: 69
Battery, the: 14
Battle Harbour: 64, 71
Battle Harbour Fun Day: 72
Battle Harbour National Historic District: 72
Bay Bulls: 25
Bay du Nord River: 46
Bay du Nord Wilderness Reserve: 46
beaches: 46, 76
Beaches Accordion Festival: 38
Belle of the Bay Inn: 29
Bell Island: 10, 29
Bell Island Gunsite: 29
Bell Island's Mine Museum and Underground Tour: 29
Beothuk Interpretation Centre: 43
berries: 67
Berry Hill Pond: 54
Big Hill Festival: 49
Big Land Fair: 79
biking: Bowring Park: 17; Fogo Island: 45; tours: 55
Birch Brook Nordic Ski Club: 78-79
Bird Cove Interpretation Centre: 57
bird-watching: Avalon Peninsula 25-26; Cape St. Mary's Ecological Reserve 28; Feather and Folk Nature Festival 61; Frenchmans Cove Provincial Park 36; Gannet Islands Ecological Reserve 75; puffins 25-26
Black Tickle: 76

boating: Avalon Peninsula 25; Bonavista 35; Bonne Bay Fjords 51; Corner Brook 49; Fogo Island and Change Island Adventure Boat Tours 45; Great Whale Coast 44; Gros Morne National Park 54; Iceberg Alley 60; to Mud Lake 81; Red Bay 71; Sandwich Bay 76; St. John's 18; Terra Nova National Park 38
Bonavista: 34
Bonavista Museum: 34
Bonne Bay Fjords: 32, 51
Bonne Bay Marine Station: 51
Bowring Park: 17
breweries: 14
Brimstone Head Folk Festival: 45
Burin Peninsula: 36-37
Burnside Heritage Foundation Archaeological Boat Tours: 38
butterflies: 47

C

cable cars: 82
Cabot Tower: 13
camping: backcountry 62; East Coast Trail 26; Gros Morne National Park 51, 56; Newman's Sound Campground 37; Notre Dame Provincial Park 40; Pinware River Provincial Park 69; St. John's 23; Terra Nova National Park 38
Canadian Side: 77-78
canoeing: 79
Cape Bonavista: 32, 34
Cape Bonavista Lighthouse Provincial Historic Site: 34
Cape Norman Lighthouse: 59
Cape Ray Lightkeeper's House: 61
Cape Shore loop: 28
Cape Spear National Historic Site: 10, 17
Cape St. George and Mainland Regional Bilingual Folk Festival: 50
Cape St. Mary's Ecological Reserve: 10, 28
C. A. Pippy Park: 15, 18
caribou: 76
Cartwright: 74
Cartwright, Captain George: 74
Castle Hill National Historic Site: 28
Cataracts Provincial Park: 27
Cercle des Mémoires: 50
Charlottetown: 37, 38

children's activities: Bonne Bay Marine Station 51; Fluvarium 17; Golden Sands Amusement Park 36; indoor glo-in-the-dark golf 42
Churchill Falls: 86, 87
Churchill Falls (Labrador) Corporation: 86
Church of the Most Holy Trinity: 34
Clarenville: 35-37
Cloud 9 Salmon Lodge: 77
Coastal Connections: 38
Coast of Bays: 46
cod, golden: 74
Colonial Building: 15
Colony of Avalon: 10, 27
Colony of Avalon Interpretation Centre: 27
comedy: 20
Conception Bay: 29
Conne River: 46
Corner Brook: 47
Corner Brook Museum and Archives: 47
Cow Head Lighthouse: 52
crab: 73
cross-country skiing: Big Land Loppet 79, 86; Birch Brook Nordic Ski Club 78-79; C. A. Pippy Park 15; Gros Morne National Park 51, 54; Labrador Open Cross Country Ski Races 86; Menihek Nordic Ski Club 86; Notre Dame Provincial Park 40; Terra Nova National Park 37
Cuckold Cove Trail: 18
Cupers Cove: 30
Cupids: 10, 29
Cupids Museum: 30
curling: 79
Curtis Memorial Hospital: 60

DE
Dee Jay Charter Boat Tours: 19
Deer Lake: 47
Discovery Centre: 52
diving: 35
dogsledding: 85
Domino: 76
Eagle River: 64, 76
Eagle River Provincial Waterway Park: 77
Eagle River Trout Lodge: 77
East Coast Trail: 26

F
Feather and Folk Nature Festival: 61
Fequet General Store: 74
Fequet Museum: 74
Ferryland: 27

Festival of Flight: 40
film festivals: 21
fishing: Happy Valley-Goose Bay 79; industry 34, 43, 52, 74, 88; Labrador City 84; lodges 77; Rigolet 88; salmon 39, 69
fjords: 51
Flagstaff Hill: 75
Fluvarium: 17
Fogo Head Trail: 45
Fogo Island: 32, 44-45
Forteau: 67
Fortune Head Ecological Reserve: 37
fossils: 27, 57
Frenchmans Cove Provincial Park: 36
French settlers: 28

G
Gallic culture: 50
Gander: 39-41
Gander Day Civic Holiday: 40
Gander International Airport: 40
Gander River boats: 39
Gannet Islands Ecological Reserve: 75
gardens: 17
Gateway to Labrador Visitor Centre: 66
Gatherall's Puffin and Whale Watch: 26
geology: 14, 37, 52
Geo Park: 10, 14
George Cartwright Monument: 75
George Street: 9, 10, 19
George Street Festival: 21
Glenn John Arts and Craft Centre: 46
Glover Island Public Reserve: 49
Golden Cod Festival: 74
Golden Sands Amusement Park: 36
golf: Bonavista 35; Corner Brook 49; Deer Lake 47; Gander 40; Grand Falls-Windsor 41; Gros Morne National Park 54; Port au Port Peninsula 50; St. John's 19
Goose Bay Airbase: 77
Government House: 15
Grand Bank: 36
Grand Bank Regional Theatre Festival: 36
Grand Bank Winter Carnival: 36
Grand Concourse Authority: 18
Grand Falls-Windsor: 41-42
Grand Lake: 32, 49
Granny's Motor Inn: 37
Great Whale Coast: 42-45
Green Gardens Trail: 54
Grenfell, Sir Wilfred: 60
Grenfell House: 60
Grenfell Interpretation Centre: 60

Gros Morne Mountain: 54
Gros Morne National Park: 47, 51-57
Gros Morne Summer Music Festival: 55
Groswater Trail: 45

H

Happy Valley-Goose Bay: 77-84
HBC Net Loft: 88
Hebron: 91
Heritage Centre: 57
Heritage Folk Festival: 38
Heritage Research Centre: 68
hiking: Appalachian Trail 62; Battle Harbour
   National Historic District 72; Bay du Nord
   Wilderness Reserve 46; Birch Brook Nordic
   Ski Club 78-79; C. A. Pippy Park 15; East
   Coast Trail 26; Fogo Island 45; Gros Morne
   National Park 51, 54; Jipujij'kuei Keuspem
   Nature Park 46; Mistaken Point Ecological
   Reserve 27; St. John's 18; Terra Nova
   National Park 37; tours 55; Twillingate 43
historic sites: Admiralty House Museum
   and Archives 18; Battle Harbour National
   Historic District 72; Cape Spear National
   Historic Site 17; Castle Hill National Historic
   Site 28; Colonial Building 15; Colony of
   Avalon 27; Cupers Cove 30; Goose Bay
   Airbase 77; Grenfell House 60; HBC Net
   Loft 88; Hopedale 90; L'Anse aux Meadows
   National Historic Site 59; Makkovik 89;
   O'Reilly House Museum 28; Quidi Vidi
   Village 14; Red Bay Historic Site 70; Ryan
   Premises National Historic Site 34
hockey: 20
Hopedale: 90
Hubbard Expedition: 82
Hudson's Bay Company: 88
hunting: Happy Valley-Goose Bay 79; Labrador
   City 84

I

Iceberg Alley: 42-45
Iceberg Festival: 60
Iceberg Quest Ocean Tours: 19, 44
icebergs: 19, 35, 71
ice sculpting: 36, 79
ice skating: 36, 79
Innu Nation: 80-81
insects: 47
Inuit Community: 88
Irish culture: 27
Irish Loop: 27

Iron Ore Company of Canada: 84
Island of Ponds: 76

JKL

Jean Lake Walking Trail: 84
Jenniex House: 51
Jipujij'kuei Keuspem Nature Park: 46
Joe Batt's Arm: 45
Johnson Geo Centre: 10, 14
Karsh, Yousuf: 29
kayaking: Gros Morne National Park 51;
   Sandwich Bay 76; Terra Nova National Park
   38; tours 55
Labrador Adventures: 67
Labrador Canoe Regatta: 79
Labrador City: 84
Labrador City town council office: 84
Labrador Culture Craft Shop: 69
Labrador Heritage Society Museum: 82
Labrador Interpretation Centre: 82
Labrador Marine: 88
Labrador Military Museum: 77
Labrador Open Cross Country Ski Races: 86
Labrador Sportsfish Ltd.: 77
Labrador Straits Museum: 68
Labrador Winter Carnival: 85
Ladies Lookout Trail: 18
Lake Melville: 81
Lamaline: 37
Lamaline Heritage Museum and Information
   Centre: 37
L'Anse Amour: 68
L'Anse au Clair: 66
L'Anse aux Meadows: 32
L'Anse aux Meadows National Historic Site: 58
lighthouses: Cape Bonavista Lighthouse
   Provincial Historic Site 34; Cape Norman
   Lighthouse 59; Cape Ray 61; Cape Spear
   National Historic Site 18; Cow Head
   Lighthouse 52; East Coast Trail 26;
   Long Point Lighthouse 43; Point Amour
   Lighthouse 68; Rose Blanche Lighthouse 62
Little Grand Lake Ecological Reserve: 49
Little Grand Lake Wildlife Reserve: 49
Loder's Point Premises Museum: 73-74
Long Point Lighthouse: 43
Long Point Trail: 43
LSPU Hall: 20

M

Makkovik: 88
Malady Head: 37, 38

Mallard Cottage Antiques and Collectibles: 14, 22
Mani Ashini Health Clinic: 81
marathons: 79
Marble Mountain: 32
Marble Mountain Resort: 50
March Hare: 49
Marconi, Guglielmo: 13, 18
Marine Atlantic: 28
Marine Services Division: 62
Maritime Archaic Burial Mound National Historic Site: 68
Mary March Provincial Museum: 41
Mary's Harbour: 73
Mary's Harbour Crab Festival: 73
Marystown: 36
Marystown Heritage Museum: 36
Marystown Hotel and Convention Centre: 36
Mealy Mountain National Park Reserve: 76
Mealy Mountains: 76
Memorial University Botanical Garden: 17
Menihek Nordic Ski Club: 64, 86
Miawpukek First Nation: 46
Mi'kmaq Craft Shop: 46
Mikmaw Discovery Centre: 46
Mile One Centre: 20
military history: 77-78
mining: 29, 84
Mistaken Point Ecological Reserve: 27
Mockbeggar Plantation: 34
Moravian settlements: 88-91
Mud Lake: 80-81
Mullowney's Puffin and Whale Tours: 26
Munday Pond Park: 17
music: Brimstone Head Folk Festival 45; Corner Brook 49; Iceberg Festival 60; Placentia Bay Cultural Arts Centre 28; St. John's 20-21; 'Striver Beach Festival 83; Twillingate/New World Island Fish, Fun, and Folk Festival 44
Muskrat Falls: 64, 83

N

Nain: 90
Native American sites/history: Beothuk Interpretation Centre 43; Burnside Heritage Foundation Archaeological Boat Tours 38; Labrador Interpretation Centre 82; Maritime Archaic Burial Mound National Historic Site 68; Mary March Provincial Museum 41; Miawpukek First Nation 46; Port au Choix 57; Sheshatshiu 80-81

Natuashish: 90
Newfoundland and Labrador Folk Festival: 21
Newfoundland Insectarium and Butterfly Pavilion: 47
Newfoundland Screech Comedy Festival: 20
Newman's Sound Campground: 37
Nickel Independent Film Festival: 21
Nicole's Picnics and Bicycle Tours: 45
Norris Point: 51, 55
Norstead Viking Village: 59
North Atlantic Aviation Museum: 32, 39
Northern Labrador: 88-91
Northern Lights: 77
Northern Peninsula: 57-60
Northern Ranger: 88
North Head Walking Trail: 18
North West River: 81
Notre Dame Provincial Park: 40

O

O'Brien's Whale and Bird Tours: 25
Old Mail Road: 54
Old Radar Base Road: 75
Oliver's Cove: 45
O'Reilly House Museum: 28
Outport Trail: 37

P

Park Lake Lodge: 77
Pentacostal Church: 89
performing arts: Gros Morne Theatre Festival 55; Happy Valley-Goose Bay 79; St. John's 20; World's End Theatre Company 45
Pinetree Line: 89
Pinware River Provincial Park: 64, 69
Placentia: 28
Placentia Area Theatre D'Heritage: 28
Placentia Bay Cultural Arts Centre: 28
Point Amour: 68
Point Amour Lighthouse: 64, 68
Polar Bear Dip: 85
polar bears: 91
Port au Choix: 32, 57
Port au Choix National Historic Site: 57
Port au Port Peninsula: 50
Port aux Basques: 61-62
Port Blandford: 37, 38
Port Hope Simpson: 74
Postville: 89
Provincial Archives: 15
Provincial Art Gallery: 15
Provincial Museum: 15

QR

Quidi Vidi Brewery: 14
Quidi Vidi Village: 9, 10, 14
rafting: 41
Railway Coastal Museum: 15
Railway Society of Newfoundland: 47
Ramea: 61
Random Passage Site: 34
RCMP detachment: 81
Red Bay: 64, 69
Red Bay Historic Site: 70
Red Bay Right Whale Exhibit: 71
remoteness: 63
Rifflin' Hitch Lodge: 77
Rigolet: 88
rock hounding: 14
Rocky Harbour: 52, 55
Rooms, The: 10, 15
Rose Blanche: 61
Rose Blanche Lighthouse: 62
Rosedale Manor: 28
rowing: 21
Royal St. John's Regatta: 21
Rugged Beauty Boat Tours: 35
Ryan Premises National Historic Site: 34

S

Saddle Island: 70
salmon fishing: 39, 69, 77
Sandwich Bay: 76
Sandy Pond: 37
scenic drives: 27
Sea of Whales Adventures: 35
Seasons in the Bight Theatre Festival: 35
Seaview Restaurant: 67
Senior Puffins Museum: 61
services: 71
Shallow Bay: 54
Sheshatshiu: 80-81
shipwrecks: 35
Signal Hill: 9, 10, 13, 18
Silent Witness Memorial: 39
Simeon Falls: 83
Sir Ambrose Shea Lift Bridge: 28
skiing: Labrador Winter Carnival 86; Marble
   Mountain Resort 50; Smokey Mountain Ski
   Lodge 86; see also cross-country skiing
Sno-Break: 79
snowboarding: 50
snowmobiling: Grand Bank Winter Carnival 36;
   Grand Falls-Windsor 41; Gros Morne National
   Park 55; Labrador Winter Carnival 85;

Mealy Mountain National Park Reserve 76;
   to Mud Lake 81; Sno-Break 79; White Wolf
   Snowmobile Club 84
Sound Symposium: 20
southern Labrador: 71-77
Southern Shore Shamrock Festival: 27
St. Alban's Inn: 46
St. Anthony: 59
St. Barbe: 57
Steady Brook Gorge: 50
Stephenville Theatre Festival: 50
St. John's: 9-25
St. John's Arts and Culture Centre: 20
St. John's Downtown Buskers Festival: 21
St. John's International Women's Film and
   Video Festival: 21
St. John's Storytelling Festival: 21
St. Lewis: 64, 73-74
St. Modeste: 69
storytelling: 21
Straits, the: 66-71
Strawberry Festival Days: 47
'Striver Beach Festival: 83
Stuckless Pond: 54
Summer Dinner Theatre: 27
Sunday Hill: 82
swimming: Bowring Park 17; Polar Bear Dip 85;
   Victoria Park 17

T

Tablelands: 52
Tablelands Trail: 52
Terra Nova National Park: 37-39
Titanic: 14
Torngat Mountains National Park: 64, 91
trains: 15, 47
Transatlantic communication: 13
TransCanada Highway: 32
Trapline Marathon: 79
Traverspine River: 83
Trinity: 34
Trinity Eco-Tours: 35
Trinity Museum: 34
Trout River: 54
Tuckamore Chamber Music Festival: 21
Twillingate: 43
Twillingate Adventure Tours: 44
Twillingate Island Boat Tours: 44
Twillingate Museum: 43
Twillingate/New World Island Fish, Fun, and
   Folk Festival: 44

UVWXYZ

UNESCO World Heritage Site: 51, 59
Victoria Park: 17
Vikings: 58
Visitor Orientation Centre: 70
Wabush: 84
Wabush Mines: 84
walking trails: Bowring Park 17; Jean Lake
    Walking Trail 84; Munday Pond Park 17
waterfalls: Cataracts Provincial Park 27;
    Churchill Falls 87; Mary's Harbour 73;
    Simeon, Muskrat and Traverspine 83-84;
    Steady Brook Gorge 50
Western Brook Pond: 52
Western Labrador: 84-87
whale-watching: Avalon Peninsula 25-26;
    Bonavista 35; Corner Brook 49; Rigolet 88;
    St. John's 18

whaling: 69-70
White Elephant Museum: 89
White Wolf Snowmobile Club: 84
Wigwam-Stuckless: 54
wildlife viewing: caribou 76; Fluvarium 17;
    Munday Pond Park 17
Winter Carnival: 49
Winterset in Summer: 38
Wintertainment: 35
Witless Bay Ecological Reserve: 25
Wonderstands: 76
Woody Point: 52, 56
World War II: 77
Wreckhouse International Jazz and Blues
    Festival: 20
Writers at Woody Point: 55
writing festivals: 52, 55
zip lines: 50

www.moon.com

DESTINATIONS | ACTIVITIES | BLOGS | MAPS | BOOKS

MOON.COM is ready to help plan your next trip! Filled with fresh trip ideas and strategies, author interviews, informative travel blogs, a detailed map library, and descriptions of all the Moon guidebooks, Moon.com is all you need to get out and explore the world—or even places in your own backyard. While at Moon.com, sign up for our monthly e-newsletter for updates on new releases, travel tips, and expert advice from our on-the-go Moon authors. As always, when you travel with Moon, expect an experience that is uncommon and truly unique.

MOON IS ON FACEBOOK—BECOME A FAN!
JOIN THE MOON PHOTO GROUP ON FLICKR

MAP SYMBOLS

▦	Expressway	◖	Highlight	✗	Airfield	⚓	Golf Course
	Primary Road	○	City/Town	✈	Airport	▣	Parking Area
	Secondary Road	◉	State Capital	▲	Mountain	▲	Archaeological Site
	Unpaved Road	◈	National Capital	✦	Unique Natural Feature	♠	Church
	Trail	★	Point of Interest			⬛	Gas Station
	Ferry	●	Accommodation	⥿	Waterfall		Glacier
	Railroad	▼	Restaurant/Bar	♠	Park		Mangrove
	Pedestrian Walkway	■	Other Location	⬛	Trailhead		Reef
	Stairs	Λ	Campground	⛷	Skiing Area		Swamp

CONVERSION TABLES

°C = (°F - 32) / 1.8
°F = (°C x 1.8) + 32
1 inch = 2.54 centimeters (cm)
1 foot = 0.304 meters (m)
1 yard = 0.914 meters
1 mile = 1.6093 kilometers (km)
1 km = 0.6214 miles
1 fathom = 1.8288 m
1 chain = 20.1168 m
1 furlong = 201.168 m
1 acre = 0.4047 hectares
1 sq km = 100 hectares
1 sq mile = 2.59 square km
1 ounce = 28.35 grams
1 pound = 0.4536 kilograms
1 short ton = 0.90718 metric ton
1 short ton = 2,000 pounds
1 long ton = 1.016 metric tons
1 long ton = 2,240 pounds
1 metric ton = 1,000 kilograms
1 quart = 0.94635 liters
1 US gallon = 3.7854 liters
1 Imperial gallon = 4.5459 liters
1 nautical mile = 1.852 km

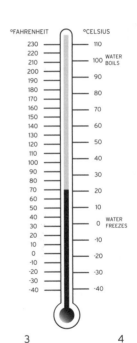

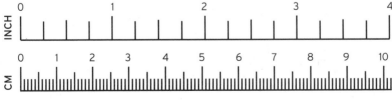